GET **HIRED**

YOUR GUIDE TO GAINING THE EMPLOYMENT YOU WANT

JULIAN PHITZROYE MARTIN II

Order this book online at www.trafford.com
or email orders@trafford.com

Most Trafford titles are also available at major online book retailers.

Print information available on the last page.

ISBN: 978-1-4907-7793-1 (sc)
ISBN: 978-1-4907-7795-5 (e)

Trafford rev. 03/01/2017

Trafford
PUBLISHING®   www.trafford.com
North America & international
toll-free: 1 888 232 4444 (USA & Canada)
fax: 812 355 4082

ACKNOWLEDGEMENTS

This book is dedicated to my creator, my mother, father, grandmother, sister, my partner and friends who have provided consistent love and support throughout this project.

By Julian Phitzroye Martin II

CONTENTS

INTRODUCTION

Hello friends and welcome to "Get Hired!" I first want to thank you for taking the time to invest in this book and in yourselves.

We all need to earn an income don't we? and preferably a very good income. It is one of the fundamental facts of life. For most of us, our primary income is derived from employment. Money in exchange for services rendered. That is at least, until we can create other ways of gaining an income. Our focus in this book is really very simple. I will, in the next few chapters, provide you with the skills and knowledge required to gain the employment and career that you seek. As I write this book, moving into a world of full globalization, free movement of labour and increased competition for employment. In these times it is important for us to sharpen up and reassess how we go about successfully securing employment. It is also worth remembering that much of the time it may be the very income from employment that will eventually allow you to create and manifest other forms of income or a business. In any case, after we have acquired the required knowledge in the form of qualifications and experience (or even if we haven't) it will be time to attempt to gain the career of our desires or employment with the company or organization of our choice.

Let me talk with you directly, like to call this "straight talk". I care about you. I care about you because I was once you. I wish I had someone to provide me with the skills and techniques I am about to relay to you, rather than to learn via trial and error, which is the most time consuming and painful way to learn. I want to save you time, I want to save you effort and I want you to avoid the pitfalls that befall so many people make as they seek employment. We all need to create an income to support ourselves and more importantly our families and we require employment to become productive members of society and our communities. We all want to be able to use our God given talents to create for ourselves a life and a career that we can be proud of. I have been through dozens of interviews, I have interviewed people myself, I have spoken with recruitment agents, with successful people in well paid careers and more importantly with people who now find themselves in employment that is both rewarding and fulfilling.

I have pooled together all of this information into an easy to comprehend pocket guide for you, which will assist you in fulfilling your career goals. So how do you obtain the career you desire? Well, it starts with acquiring the first position of employment. But, how do we get the first position? Very simply put, by convincing the appropriate parties at the desired company or organization to hire us. This usually means presenting a stunning impression of ourselves within some form of interview process. Within this book, we are concerned with the phases involved in gaining employment and there are a number of factors which will have an influence, we will explore these factors in the coming chapters.

I have been through many job interviews in my lifetime and with the help of other interview veterans and in depth research I able now able to provide you with a concise handbook to help you conduct and successfully complete the interview and employment process. In short I am showing you how to get your perspective employers to say the words "You Are Hired!"

This handbook has been constructed to be a reference for you, so you may delve into any of the chapters whenever you wish. It can be used weeks before or even hours before the interview. Be aware that some of the information and techniques may seem new to you. Try to carry out the tasks and suggestions in full because they are tried and tested techniques which have proven over and over again to be a fundamental part of successfully completing an interview and employment process. Using these techniques will enable you to eventually gain the full time employment of your choice.

Out of the box thinking may be required as well as repetition, but rest assured "IF YOU FOLLOW THE GUIDANCE IN THIS BOOK TO THE LETTER, YOU WILL BE SUCCESSFUL!"

Further, I will say that once mastered, you will be able to pass on this knowledge to your friends and loved ones. So let us begin our journey friends and learn the ways and methods of the successful ones, get a comfortable chair and journey with me through the corridors of knowledge. Are you ready to get hired? Good, then let us begin.......

Words of Wisdom:

> *"The problems we face today cannot be solved at the same level of thinking we were at time when we created them."*

Albert Einstein

CHAPTER 1

The Correct State of Mind

Welcome to the first chapter, I'm glad that you have decided to empower yourself and I want to encourage you to stay the course and use the information in this book to improve your skills and knowledge to Get Hired!

Most of us want to be successful in life and if you are reading this book then it is my assumption that you want to be a success at gaining the career of your dreams. But first let us define what success is, The Oxford Dictionary defines success as "the accomplishment of an aim, purpose or goal". As part of my research prior to writing this book it was necessary for me to look at the area of success and how individuals gain the ability and skills to achieve their goals. I have through my research identified 3 key components to success in any endeavor which I will reveal shortly. So before we even begin on our journey together it is important that we have packed the appropriate provisions. Before we build our house we know that we must create a strong and durable foundation. We also know that if we want anything in life we need to be totally clear about our purpose or aim or goal, if we don't we tend to become distracted and eventually without a sense of direction inevitably we become disillusioned.

So, since you're reading this book I believe it is safe to assume that your aim or purpose is to create for yourself the career of your choice. With any aim just by being clear about our purpose we have already won half of the battle. In addition, if we are going to be successful we would also require a plan or strategy to obtain our goal. The successful accomplishment of any goal in life requires a strategy. It doesn't matter whether we are studying for an exam, looking for a life partner or even a nation going to war, it all requires strategy. You will be glad to know that by reading this book you already have the strategy; you already have a step by step guide to success. It seems then, that we have identified two of our components for success, the first is a clear goal and the second is a strategy. The third is what I would like to talk to you about in a little more detail because without it I am afraid that success may elude you. Now, the third component marks the difference in life between ultimate success and or inevitable failure. It has been called by many names over the ages, belief, faith, persistence but in essence it is quite simple. It is the basis for all action, 'the correct state of mind'. By the correct state of mind, I mean what is going on inside your head.

Our mind is an extremely powerful creation; it is defined by the Oxford Dictionary as "the element of a human being that enables them to be aware of the world and experiences, to think and to feel. It is the faculty of consciousness and thought". The mind controls our thoughts and eventually everything that we do. This is an extremely important point to consider before moving forward. Your mind is the master of your universe, every technique that you will learn within this book will require you to use your mind more effectively. This will as a consequence improve your results. All of our outer circumstances are a product of our thinking and the creation of a career and the appropriation of employment is absolutely no different. We must, if we are to be successful, enter the interview with the correct psychology, which is a state of mind. With regard to the correct psychology we must be aware that there are a number of areas to consider and I will be guiding you through them one by one. So fear not, by the end of this you will have the tools that you need. You will have the tools to be successful and obtain your desired goal.

Let me ask you a simple question. What do you think marks the difference between the two men I am about to describe? Let's call them Mark and Matthew. Mark and Matthew both used to work

2

together at the same company as office administrators and due to a recession, both have been made redundant and are out of work. Both Mark and Matthew are now looking for employment. Mark is looking for a job and he applies for two roles every week. After his continuous applications are rejected for 6 weeks he becomes naturally disheartened and decides that maybe there are no jobs for him. Mark gives up. Eventually Mark decides to seek unemployment benefit and remains on the state welfare system for the foreseeable future. Matthew is also looking for a job. Matthew applies to two jobs every day. After 6 weeks of continuous rejection he too is faced with the same problem. So Matthew makes a decision. Matthew triples the amount of applications he is making from two jobs a day to six per day. A threefold increase. In addition, he begins to read books like this one (Get Hired), on improving his employment seeking skills. After two more weeks he again doubles his applications, this time to twelve applications per day and in addition he attends career workshops and seminars. Eventually he is successful and obtains his ideal role.

What was the difference between Mark and Matthew? What was it that made them take the actions that they did? The difference my friends is quite simply, The State of Mind. Our imaginary characters Mark and Matthew are working with two very different states of mind. Mark was hoping. Matthew was determined, for him it was a must! This important foundation must be established before we move forward with understanding and employing the strategies to create our dream career. Firstly, consider that certain conditions can and will affect your mind and its current state. We shall cover these different states of minds or 'mind-states' shortly. The mind is either in a positive state or a negative state, there is no in-between. You may ask quite fairly, how do I know what state of mind I am in? And I would answer you by saying that certain attributes or feelings are present depending on to what state you are in. So, if you are in a positive state of mind or 'peak state' you will experience some of the following feelings, high energy, happiness, excitement, motivation or intense desire, enthusiasm, clarity, contentment, passion and there are of course others.

If you are not feeling at least one or more of these feelings it is highly likely that you are in a negative state of mind or an "unresourceful state", again this state also has symptoms which will include, anxiety, worry, tiredness, apathy, boredom, fear, confusion, anger, sadness, uncertainty and there are others. These feelings are clear symptoms of our current state of mind. Now that we know which symptoms are present for each state of mind, we should ask ourselves what exactly can influence our psychology or state of mind. Through my research I have come to understand that there are only two real effectors of a human being's state of mind and these are physiology and thoughts. Physiology relates to the state of physical being. Thoughts relate to the image, pictures, thoughts or ideas that you are currently holding in your mind. These are the only two factors, once we can completely control these then we can control our outcomes.

A: Physiology Explained

Firstly, our physiology effect's our state of mind, so the first thing to understand is how to change our physiological state. This is especially important not just for interviews but the whole employment process. Remember the amount of oxygen in the blood going to the brain and the muscle tension within your body will eventually all effect the mind. We have to keep ourselves in a state that will increase energy and oxygen to the brain and body for optimum performance.

A1: Breathing:

Correct breathing is extremely important. You need to be able to breathe deep breaths in through the nose and out through the mouth. Eight or so of these will make you feel calm if you are nervous and also allow your body and particularly your brain access to the oxygen it needs to function at the optimum level.

A2: Muscle Movement:

Next, we need to lose the tension in our bodies. Stretching your arms and legs and shaking them out is enough to reduce the stiffness and allow the blood to flow more freely through our bodies. Stretching is very important for refreshing ourselves and releasing tension.

B: Psychology Explained

Now one of the key steps to your success is to enter any interview in what we can call a 'peak state' or 'state of certainty'. Now my dear friends, what I mean by these phrases is a psychological state of absolute confidence. We must put ourselves in a state of complete confidence, belief, power and energy. We need to be able to give the performance of our lives.

B1: Visualization

The process of visualization is extremely powerful. This process involves us creating a picture of an event or series of events within our minds. You will need to relax in a quiet place and it is usually best to close your eyes. Then, in your mind you need to create a view (a picture comprised of moving images), for example if we were visualizing our successful interview we would see ourselves walking into the interview room, sitting down, meeting the interviewer, shaking hands and answering the questions successfully. You need to create a view as if you were looking through your own eyes or watching it. The more we rehearse the scenario the more easily we will be able perform a similar set of actions in real life.

B2: Affirmation

The process of affirmation allows us to condition an idea or command into our minds, it is a form of mind programming. An affirmation is a carefully formed statement that we repeat to ourselves either in our mind or out loud.

An affirmation is a positive statement such as 'Every day I grow more confident and enthusiastic!', typically it is said with authority and conviction and repeated numerous times 10-15 typically. This process repeated over time literally programs the mind to behave in the way the statement has ordered.

How to induce the Correct State of Mind?

The combination of vigorous movement, visualization and seeing the goal already accomplished will help to induce the correct state of mind (incidentally music is also useful but we shall stick to natural methods for now). You must follow these processes to the letter to be successful and induce the required peak state.

The Method:

Execute the follow the following steps:

First, stretch lightly and shake out your body. Now begin to breathe in deeply through your nose and out through your mouth. Next, begin to create in your mind the picture of being in the interview. See it as if you were looking through your own eyes. You should see the interview going very well, the interviewer smiling at your answers and nodding in agreement as you answer each question fully and to absolute perfection. As your visualization continues and you move forward in time, move your body more and more vigorously, stretch, jump a little, jog lightly on the spot, do whatever you need to do to increase your circulation, energy and excitement in your body. Continue the visualization, start to smile, think of something funny, giggle, and laugh.

......Very Good!

Now we must see the goal accomplished. So see the interviewer offering you the job and accept the job out load. Thank the interviewer, smile and be confident in accepting the offer. This exercise may seem ridiculous to the common man, but trust me I have used this process myself many times and I have never failed a job interview in my life. This process of visualization is of enough importance as to warrant a whole chapter for itself, but what I am giving you here my friends are the essential parts. The idea behind visualizing is that the more the mind can rehearse a specific set of actions the more accurately it can carry out those actions in real life.

Visualization or mental rehearsal is a pre-requisite of success in all areas and the job interview is no different. This is the basic run-through that you must do before the interview. Go to the toilet/restroom if you have to or somewhere quiet where you'll not be seen. You have the tools now so repeat this process many times before the interview in the days and weeks before and just before. Remember that repetition is the mother of skill, so keep practicing this exercise over and over again. This tool is a trick that will help you without a doubt to become more confident and induce the correct state of mind.

Words of Wisdom:

"Nothing great was ever achieved without enthusiasm".

Ralph Waldo Emerson

CHAPTER 2

The S.A.I. Process and Preparation

So my friends, we have learned and understood how to change our state of mind in order to give us the best possible chance of success as we begin to generate our dream careers and of course eventually, Get Hired!

There is an old saying that you may have heard before which states that 'All wars and battles are won or lost before they even start'. Well, the realization of a dream career is also a type of battle, or at the very least it is a challenging situation in which we need to understand what is required and what to prepare for. That is to say, if we desire success it is likely that the majority of the work required will take place even before we enter into the interview, including already being in the correct state of mind as we discussed within Chapter 1: The Foundation. My aim in this chapter, is to ensure that you understand the type of preparation required and are ready to do battle. So how are we to prepare? How will we prepare in such a way as to make ourselves almost certain of victory in our task? How do we prepare for our task of gaining the employment of our choice? Firstly, before we even start we need to look at what we are preparing for and we need to understand the stages involved in acquiring the career of our choice. Broadly, we can say that the process of acquiring employment is divided into three areas which we call S.A.I. The three areas are The Search, The Application and The Interview.

Incidentally my friends, you will notice that as we move through these chapters I will always separate the elements of any process or block of knowledge into its appropriate parts. The purpose is to allow you to focus on specific areas and in addition to have clarity and map how far you have come and what else there is to do. Now back to The S.A.I. Process, we need to understand the elements of S.A.I. and then to make the appropriate preparations for the completion of each of these phase so let us first briefly define exactly what they are. The search is basically the process of finding a job to apply for. The second step once we have found a suitable position is to make an application for it and have it accepted. The third and final step is of course to attend the interview, impress the interviewers and obtain the role. Sounds simply enough doesn't it? Then why do so many people fail miserably at this process? From my observations and research, it is clear to me that most people are simply not clear on all the elements of the process which would have ensured their success and they do not make the correct preparation. It's time for us then to look at S.A.I. in more detail and then to gain an understanding of exactly what to do.

The Search Process:

The first element to consider in the search process is the object or aim of our search. We need to be clear of exactly what we are looking for. What you need to define is what type of role you want. I cannot stress enough the importance of this element. Ask yourselves the Nine Criteria Questions. The nine questions provide us with a clear guide which will allow us to be specific about our search and guide us to the appropriate position which will be in line with our goals and aspirations.

It will be almost impossible to find employment and subsequently create our dream career without answering the Nine Criteria Questions (NCQ). Performing this step is a must my friends, a must for those who want success. All people who now have their dream careers have asked of themselves the NCQ.

The NCQ are listed below:

The NCQ Process

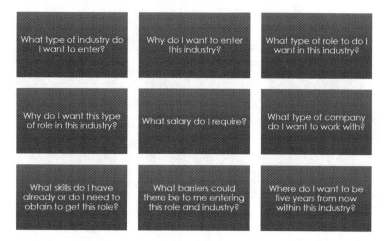

| What type of industry do I want to enter? | Why do I want to enter this industry? | What type of role to do I want in this industry? |
| What skills do I have already or do I need to obtain to get this role? | What barriers could there be to me entering this role and industry? | Where do I want to be five years from now within this industry? |

Once you have answered the NCQ, we have established for ourselves the blueprint for our search. If you are unsure about NCQ do not worry because I will later provide you with an example. This is all a part of the appropriate preparation. The NCQ Process has provided us with the blueprint for our search and we are now able to judge any of the employment roles we find by the answers to the Nine Criteria Questions. In addition, we can mark based on the NCQ how well the role in question matches up with what we are looking for. We can even provide a mark out of ten if we desire.

Now that we have completed our initial stage let us move on.

We are now clear about what we are looking for but now we have to be able to find what we are looking for and we need to know the best way to do this. I will now provide you with some techniques to locate the employment positions. There are of course many ways to seek and find employment roles, but I will reveal to you from my research the top seven. These are called the Seven Search Techniques or SST. Incidentally you will notice that each process I am revealing to you I have also given a shorthand or abbreviation of so that is easy to remember and later I will provide you with a roadmap of the stages to simplify this for you.

The Seven Search Techniques (The SST Process)

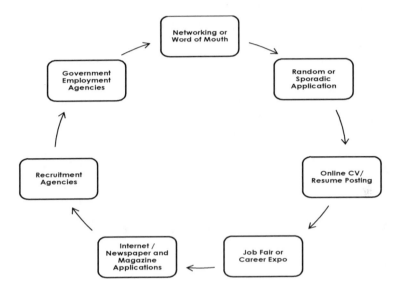

In order to be successful it is imperative that you complete the SST Process. If you miss out any of the above, then you will not have given yourself the best chance and I cannot guarantee for you success and that is the entire point of this process and all of the knowledge contained within this book. My friends, the SST process works! It is a tried and tested methodology. Complete the entire SST to ensure yourself success! Let me explain to you in a little more detail each of the search techniques so that you are able to execute them all with precision.

1: Job Fair or Career Expo:

A job fair or career expo is a fair or exposition where employers, recruiters, government agencies and schools meet with prospective job seekers. Expos usually include company or organization tables or booths where resumes /CV's can be collected and business cards can be exchanged. Career Expo's are good places to meet many company representatives from organizations and corporations of all industries and sizes within a short period of time. Be aware friends, that by using this system you will be meeting members of the perspective employers face to face and so you will need to be prepared and ready to interact socially. We will look at interpersonal skills later in the book, but it is safe to say here that at the very least you should be dressed appropriately.

2: Internet / Newspaper and Magazine Applications:

You will find that most organizations these days post their job vacancies on employment websites which is a web site dealing specifically with employment or careers. Many employment websites are designed to allow employers to post job requirements for a position to be filled and are commonly known as job boards. The advantage of using employment websites is the sheer volume of vacancies available including international job positions. In addition, you will find the more traditional avenues such as industry magazines and newspapers are excellent places to look. In the case of newspapers, usually they will have job postings for certain industries on specific days so it is important to keep abreast of the schedule.

3: Recruitment Agencies:

If you want a little more assistance with your employment search, then recruitment agencies can offer additional support because you have another group of people actively working on your behalf. A recruitment agency acts as a direct contact between companies and organizations (employers) and the job candidates they recruit (prospective employees). Recruitment agents charge the companies they are working on the behalf of a fee for finding the appropriate candidate based on the criteria provided by the employer.

4: Networking or Word of Mouth:

This technique requires you to utilize your own circle of family, friends, associates and acquaintances to spread the word around that you are looking for employment in a certain area. This part of the process requires you to be extremely proactive and sociable. People that you are associated with may be aware of vacancies available in their places of work and of course will in addition, be able to put in a good word for you or act as an official reference.

5: Random or Sporadic Application:

We need to remember that not all job roles are advertised. Indeed, the statistics suggest that only 40% of available job roles are advertised. Remember dear reader that, you do not need to wait for a role to be advertised before you apply to the prospective organization. Why wait for them? Many firms will consider an application from a good candidate and indeed many organizations are at this moment 'thinking about expanding'. If you are proactive you can beat your competition and be the first in line, remember that the universe favors those that take action.

6: Online CV / Resume Posting:

A great way to gain exposure is to post your CV/resume online and let people find you. That is to say that you can advertise yourself. One of the most effective ways to gain maximum and global exposure is to post you CV/resume online. This can be done on one of the many recruitment websites available online where companies and recruitment agencies will be able to locate you. Of course, you need to ensure that you have the most up-to-date version of your CV / Resume available online. In addition, in the same vein, it is also possible to create your own website showcasing your skills and you CV in more detail.

7: Government Employment Agencies:

The governments of most countries also have employment agencies, which are organizations specifically designed to move the domestic unemployed population back into employment. Government employment agencies are not profit orientated and you may find the availability of positions more limited in scope, however they are still an important part of SST Process. Usually you are required to make applications in person initially before you are able to search via their online systems. My friends, I hope this has provided you with a good overview of the elements of the SST Process, remember SST is a process and every element must be completed if we are to ensure maximum opportunities to be available to us and ensure our success. Once we have completed SST and have a selection of positions it is time to move to the next stage.... the application process.

The Application Process:

Now that we have completed SST Process and have been persistent, we should have found some employment positions to make an application to. There are a number of ways to apply for a role but almost all will involve either filling in an application form of more likely sending the prospective employer your CV / Resume. An application form will ask you a series of questions about yourself and some which relate to the role you are applying for. Examples would be name, address, academic record, employment history. You will need to fill the form in fully. The key is to fill the form with the following considerations:

- Use neat hand writing,
- Use the correct spelling and grammar
- Use excellent punctuation
- Answer all the questions fully, but be concise

It may be the case that the position requires you to apply using a CV / Resume. In this case one of two letters must accompany the CV / Resume. You will send either a Speculative Letter or a Cover Letter. A speculative letter is used when you are applying to an organization that has not advertised a vacancy. The speculative letter provides an overview of the contents of your CV / Resume and in addition requests that your CV/Resume may be considered for any positions in a certain area specified by you. Also, within the speculative letter you will provide evidence of why you are suitable for the role. The cover letter is sent along with your application for an advertised position as a way of introducing yourself to potential employers and explaining your suitability for the desired position.

Details such as qualifications, work experience and academic achievements are included along with the appropriate dates and locations. In addition, you will be required to send your CV / Resume to the prospective employer. I will in subsequent chapters go into more detail regarding these application documents and provide good examples and advice. A CV / Resume is usually one to three pages long, a typical résumé contains a summary of relevant job experience and education. You will need to send both the covering letter and CV ensuring you have covered the relevant areas.

The Interview Process:

The Interview is the final stage of the SAI Process. An interview is a conversation between two or more people (the interviewer and the interviewee) where questions are asked by the interviewer to obtain information from the interviewee. Of course, the questions will relate to the employment position being applied for and the validity of your application and suitability for the role in question. We will deal with the interview in much more detail later in this book but the main area I want us to focus on here is that of preparation. Specifically, the area of preparation we need to look at is practice. We must practice. The old adage still rings true, 'practice makes perfect'. Before we move forward to the last stage of the SAI Process which is the interview we must ensure that we know exactly what we are going to do and say. Quite simply we must rehearse. What we need to do is go through the whole interview process in real life like an actor practices and rehearses his part in a play. This is very different from what we have learnt in the previous chapter, there we were concerned with practice through visualization, but here we a going to be going through the real life process. We need conduct to the interview in advance as if we were already there.

Now, we live in an age of technology and we must utilize that technology to our own benefit because technology can assist us in our tasks. Camcorders are a useful tool as we can record ourselves carrying out the interview in advance without risk and therefore pick and choose the areas of our presentation that we deem to be advantageous and change the ones that are not. So firstly, we must set the scene. What we are going to do is rehearse the whole affair. For this it is a good idea to dress in exactly the same clothing as you would within the real interview. You are able to get an idea of appropriate clothing from Chapter 3. It is best if you are able, to practice with a friend who will be able to play the part of the interviewer and ask a series of questions in the style of a tough interview. Using a desk between you and with note paper in hand you should rehearse the whole affair from the initial handshake and small talk straight through to the question and answer section and finally the close of the interviews. I have provided for you a list of appropriate questions that you can expect in Chapter 4 and these will enable you to construct the appropriate answers.

Of course, we need to be aware that in real life the interviewer may approach you with any manner of questions, in any order. When rehearsing, care should be taken to be as unpredictable with the questioning as possible. You are preparing in order to be ready for any question. Remember friends this is supposed to allow you to identify areas that you are weak on. It may be worth having a few practice sessions before you beginning filming. If you do not have a recording devise to use the you can borrow or buy one. Now, my friends there are many key areas that most people tend to overlook. These are the areas within the interview that can let us down and I would now like to identify certain areas and stay aware of the following areas listed below. Obviously, once you have conducted the interview the idea is to stop the recording, rewind and then review.

Whilst completing the practice interview pay attention for the following:

1) How much energy are you displaying when you speak, is it high in energy or low?
2) Are you leaning forward or backwards?
3) Are speaking fast or slowly?
4) How in depth are your answers, are you going into detail or skimming?
5) Look at your posture, is it stiff or relaxed, are you slouching or upright.

6) You may be able to notice your breathing if you look carefully, is it shallow or is it deep (remember deeper breathes increase oxygen flow to the brain and increase productivity of your bio-system and induce a peak state).

7) Are you using hand gestures to explain yourself or are you relying on vocals.

8) What is the volume of your vocal communication, is it loud or quiet, clear or muffled?

9) Are you looking your interviewer in the eye?

10) Are you nodding and displaying movements associated with active listening while your interviewer speaks to you?

11) How long are you taking to answer the question? Is there a long pause between answers?

12) Are you smiling or are you straight faced?

13) How was your rapport building skills in the initial few seconds and minutes when you first began the interview? Did you make small talk?

14) Are you displaying any warmth or are you robotic?

15) Are you using slang in your speech or peppering your talk with phrases such as "umm", "err", "you know", "you get me", "understand". (This can be irritating to even the most tolerant of interviewers).

16) How are you answering the question with enthusiasm or restraint?

Now my friends, there are no wrong or right answers to the above questions and you can use your intuition as to what you believe are the correct responses. But let me at least offer you some general directions in terms of what you should do. You as an interviewee should be energetic, engaging, upbeat in demeanor, clear when speaking, expressive (within reason) and warm. Remember the idea is to make the interviewer like us, it is important to see the interview from the other person's point of view. That is, the interviewer will usually be thinking 'can I work alongside this person comfortably or will they fit into the company well?'.

This section should have given you an idea of what to look out for when you are reviewing your interview tape. My friends, be aware that repetition is the mother of skill and that the more you practice the closer you will come to perfection. I would personally recommend at least ten such tries and reviews to ensure a good real life interview and please my friends remember to vary the questions and how they are presented, as it is easy to fall into the trap of predictability. You can do this!

Good luck guys.

Words of Wisdom:

"Habits are first cobwebs, then ropes".

African Proverb

CHAPTER 3

Presentation

Hello and welcome to the 3rd Chapter. I want first of all to commend you on your dedication. Did you know that 70% of people who buy a book never read past the first chapter? So well done and keep going, you're doing great! Soon you will Get Hired!

In the last chapter we began to touch upon the interview process. I want to look at a specific aspect of the interview process which we need to master if we are to be successful in our search for our dream job or career. Fortunately, or unfortunately in life appearances do matter. We are judged on how we look and research tells us that the majority of people make a judgment based on appearances within the first 5 seconds of meeting someone. The job interview is no different, we must remember that from the first moments of the interview we will be judged on our appearance long before we open our mouths. Just think for a moment about the typical series of people that you will encounter when attending an interview. You will arrive at the premises and the security guard will be the first to see you, followed swiftly by the receptionist, then the assistant of whoever is interviewing you and then finally the interviewer and there may be more than one of him or her.

It is safe to say that each of the individuals listed previously will consciously or unconsciously make a judgement of you and absent of conversation this will be based primarily on your appearance therefore we need to be extremely careful about how we appear and what we wear. Our aim, even before we attend the interview is to have clear in our minds that our appearance is going to influence those individuals whom we meet. Luckily, we have full control over this. We can use appearance to our advantage. So let us have a look at appearance. In a study published in 1994, Dr. Jeff Biddle and Daniel Hamermesh compared the results of three surveys, two of them Canadian and one American. The surveys looked at how people were perceived in interviews and how the look of someone could affect results. The surveys were conducted by government agencies in their respective countries and consisted of questions asked regarding the income, occupation, background of interviewees and the ratings of the attractiveness of interviewees by their interviewers.

The attractiveness of the interviewees was rated on a five-point scale ranging from 'homely' to 'handsome or beautiful', with points in between for 'below average', 'average', and 'above average'. Biddle and Hamermesh found that the combined results of the surveys 'make it clear that there is a significant penalty for bad looks among men'. One Biddle and Hamermesh 1994 study showed that the 9 percent of working men who were rated by interviewers as either 'homely' or 'below average' in physical appearance also received 9 percent less than average in terms of hourly earnings. By contrast, the 32 percent of men who were rated 'above average' or 'handsome' by interviewers earned 5 percent more than the average for men in the sample. Attractiveness is of course in the eye of the beholder. However, we can change how we look and therefore influence how we are perceived. Let's look at another example of appearance.

This is an excerpt from a magazine called Psychology Today printed on November 1st 1997, it reads:

"Psychologists have persuasively demonstrated that in court attractive defendants are perceived as more credible, are acquitted more often, and receive lighter sentences than their less appealing counterparts... Judges and juries can be swayed by more than just a pretty face, the clothing defendants wear, the jewelry they display, the way they style their hair, can sometimes mean the difference between doing time and dodging jail."

Jury consultants, often trained in both psychology and law, counsel their clients on how to speak, when to gesture—and not least, what to wear. "The jury is going to form impressions of you based on subtle characteristics of personality and attitude, and dress is one important element," says Robert Gordon, a Dallas-based psychologist and jury consultant. I will now provide you with a step by step guide on providing the most eye pleasing appearance for your employment meeting or interview with your prospective employer. There are two sections below which will provide an outline. Remember these are not hard and fast rules and the attire that is appropriate will differ depending on the type of business and also the culture of the organization. I shall keep this short and to the point for you as this is a simple matter of correct dress.

Here are guides below for both male and female:

Presentation Dress Code Guides:

Hair:

Men: The best style is short and neat. Clean shaven, no beards. If you have long hair, then pull back in a ponytail. No wild hair do's, please avoid hairstyles that can be interpreted as aggressive.

Women: The style of your hair should not be too fussy, no crazy hair dye colors i.e. bright green, bright pink, stick to your natural color if possible. Highlights are ok as long as they are simple and classy. Please, no punk rocker hair styles and nothing extreme. Conservative style is best at this stage. Examples of this would be, neat braids, hair pulled back in a ponytail, hair clipped up, combed down away from the face.

Accessories / Jewelry:

Men: No earrings should be worn; rings should be kept to one each per hand. Simple smart watches are best, nothing extravagant.

Women: Subtle and conservative jewelry is allowed, pearls and studs. But nothing dangly, no 'bling-bling' please. For the ladies, please keep the number of rings down to one for each hand at the maximum.

Dress code:

Men: Always wear a suit, the best colors are dark ones. Dark blue, black and grey. Other louder colors should be avoided if possible.

Women: Smart clothes are essential. A tailored suit is advisable either with trousers or knee length skirts, the colors which are preferable are black or dark blue with a crisp white shirt. For example, a smart blouse with either trousers or a skirt.

Shoes:

Men: Simple black leather or brown is best, lace ups rather than slip-on's.

Women: Flat shoes or medium heels are preferable. Nothing over the top. Remember to always pay attention to the type of organization that you are applying for. What I mean is that, a job as a fashion designer might be more lenient to extravagant dress for the interview than an accountancy firm, they may even encourage it. In general, the interviewer will be looking for someone who can represent their business in the best possible way and act as a professional. One of the ways in which we can influence our prospective employer to the fact that they have indeed found that person in us, is to create the correct image.

Perfume and Cologne:

Your scent (even if you smell good) can be an issue. Remember that smell is one of the strongest senses and your favorite perfume or cologne might be the same scent the interviewer's ex-wife or ex-husband wore. That subliminal negative impact could squash your chances of getting a job offer. With any type of scent, less, simple or none, is better.

What not to wear at an interview:

- Flip-flops or sneakers
- Underwear (bras, bra straps, briefs, boxers, etc.) that is visible
- Shorts
- Jeans
- Skirts that are too short
- Pants that are too low-rise or too tight
- Blouses that are too low-cut or too short—don't show your cleavage or your belly

In addition to the above, please remember that if you are applying to roles within Islamic countries or institutions your dress sense will need to be much more conservative, especially for women. Therefore, do the required research to gain an understanding of the cultural norms.

I hope this has given you some practical guidance on presentation my friends, now let us move on to other important areas such as….

Words of Wisdom:

"Beauty is everywhere a welcome guest."

Johann Wolfgang von Goethe

CHAPTER 4

Interview Questions and Answers

There will be a time eventually when you must attend the interview, and you will be asked a number of questions. These questions are asked of you to test who you are and what you know. Interviews are a battle of skill just like any other game such as chess or monopoly and therefore we must rise to the challenge. I will now provide you with some examples of the types of questions that you may be asked and some guidance as to how they can be answered skillfully. You may also like to use these examples if and when you conduct you taped role play session from Chapter 2.

The questions and answers are as follows:

What do you like most about this job/role?

Explain and give examples about your enthusiasm for the particular profession or role. Comment on wanting to do a first-rate job. Say what you hope to achieve and why.

What kind of experience do you have for this job?

Talk about your past jobs roles, but relate them to the present job role. Gather information about the companies before answering. Ask what projects or activities you would be working on in the first six to twelve months. Apply your experiences to those projects, detailing exactly how you would go about completing the required tasks.

How long would it take you to make a contribution to our company?

Ask the interviewer to explain which areas need the greatest contribution, perhaps focusing on a specific area. Provide a realistic timeline, but express confidence of an almost immediate contribution which will increase dramatically over time. Show step by step how long it would take you to get settled and get working—the quicker, the better.

What are your qualifications?

Clarify the questions; ask if he /she requires evidence of academia and training or job-related qualifications. Also ask what specific projects or problems you may be expected to deal with. Relate all qualifications you have to the role and what is required. Give examples of their application. Mention teamwork and the important of co-workers being able to reply on each other.

How do you go about preparing for presentations?

Discuss your system of preparation. Provide a specific example. Give examples of successful presentations.

Has a supervisor ever challenged one of your decisions? How did you respond?

Discuss an example where you supported your decision with research or analytical data. Show that even though you supported your decision, you were open to suggestions or comments.

Have you ever misjudged something? How could you have prevented the mistake?

Briefly discuss a specific but minor example. Focus more on what you learnt than on the actual mistake.

What extracurricular activities do you partake in? What leadership positions did you hold? Why didn't you or have you not partaken in more extracurricular activates?

Discuss all hobbies and roles outside work, focus on leadership roles, teamwork, and self-motivation; explain how those experience will help you in the job role. Talk about any hobbies you have any why you like them. If you have few or none explain how dedication to your job has at times impacted other areas of your life, because of your unrelenting dedication, however mention that you understand and are beginning to achieve more balance.

What types of position are you interested in and why?

Describe the position for which you're interviewing. This area is usually clear before the interview, however be prepared for the interviewer to ask this, especially if they are currently hiring for multiple positions. Be specific about what you're looking for (you must not seem to be happy to take just any positive even if you are). Explain how that position will help you reach your career goals.

Can you work overtime and on weekend?

Discuss your commitment to the job and the extra time you're willing to put into it.

Use terms that proclaim your motivation and recent dedication.

Were you fired from your last job?

If it was your fault:

Say you learned an enormous lesson during the experience. Explain you messed up, but you learnt a valuable lesson and now won't make the same mistakes again. Explain briefly how you benefited from this learning experience. Discuss the benefits of learning through mistakes.

If it was not your fault:

Explain the firing as a result of downsizing, mergers, company closure, or some other act beyond your control. Sometimes firing happens several times in a row to good hardworking people due to circumstances. These questions are fairly general but some variation of the questions above will almost without a doubt come up within the interview. Therefore, it's again a good idea to practice the answers to these questions and come up with alternative answers and practice, practice, practice.

Good Luck, you are slowly becoming an interview master!

Words of Wisdom:

"One today is worth two tomorrows".

Benjamin Franklin

CHAPTER 5

Correct Language

Welcome to Chapter 5 my friends.

I'm so happy you are on this journey with me and I hope your finding it useful. The skills that you are learning in these chapters will empower you to get the job of your choice and create the career of your dreams. As I have mentioned previously throughout this book I am providing you with the key knowledge on each area that you need to master in order to obtain the employment of your choice, do something you love and create your dream career. As I keep repeating to you, I want you to hear the words "You Are Hired!" and experience the joy of having accomplished your goal. In order to obtain absolutely anything in life we need to communicate. We need to express ourselves in a way that can be understood very clearly to other people. All forms of trade involve communication. All transference of information and knowledge requires communication. The process of obtaining our dream career is no different. In the previous chapter we looked at how our appearance communicates messages to the people around us. Now it is time to focus on verbal communication.

We first need to understand the principles of effective verbal communication and then to put them into practice. We communicate verbally through the use of language and we need to master the art of correct language. Verbal communication is likely to take place in a number of situations during the process of obtaining employment. At the application stage it may be in the form of a career expo or interview with a recruitment agency or government employment agency. If you are making random applications to companies who have not advertised a position this may require making a telephone call and introducing yourself. Later in the process, at the interview stage a telephone interview for instance may take place and eventually verbal communication skills will be needed in the face to face interviews. In all of these situations whoever you are speaking with will be assessing you and building an impression of you based on your verbal communication and so we must employ the use of correct language. Language influences people and I want you to take a closer look at this area.

Communication and how language influences:

Firstly, I shall provide you with some background knowledge in the area of language and its application to serve as a foundation for your learning. Correct language is really a language that is made up of words that have a powerful impression on people's minds. Correct language is made up of words that bring out emotion and thoughts in people. They can be used to induce particular types of action. We need to first understand the human mind has two parts, the conscious mind and the subconscious mind.

The Conscious Mind

The Conscious Mind is the aspect of our mental processing that is inside of our awareness. It is the mind that we can think and talk about in a rational way.

The Subconscious Mind

The Subconscious Mind is the aspect of the mind we are largely unaware of. This is the part of the mind that regulates your breathing and heartbeat, but in addition it also includes unconscious feelings, unconscious or automatic skills, unconscious thoughts, unconscious habits and automatic reactions, complexes, hidden phobias and concealed desires. The subconscious mind can be in influenced by language and can be greatly influenced by the correct language. So let's go a little deeper. Correct language uses patterns of language that bypass conscious reasoning and speak directly to the subconscious mind. This language influences people at the subconscious level. This allows you to direct people to take specific actions or have certain thoughts. The mind is always analyzing what's going on around it and processing information. Your subconscious mind has stored thousands of conversations with other human beings.

These conversations have become so routine that you don't even realize you are registering and storing them. Your own subconscious mind runs on auto-pilot. It's accustomed to remembering or responding to information day after day. It looks for patterns. When using correct language, we are creating patterns that force the subconscious mind to wake up and pay attention. Well, what is the result? The subconscious receives a direct and specific command that it feels compelled to act on. Let me explain. In a normal, everyday conversation an investor or bank communicate with their customers and potential customers. They can influence them to sell a house, sign a deed, sign a contract, accept an offer, or whatever it is else you want them to do with absolutely no resistance.

How & why is there no resistance?

Correct language bypasses conscious reasoning and speaks directly to the subconscious level. We use correct language to create commands. The command simply begins to penetrate the minds of the receiver and in this way you can get them to do whatever it is you want them to do or at least heavily influence their decisions. Correct language commands are one to four word groups that order you to do something, and they make sense on their own. Commands are like time bombs. When you use a command, you don't instantly see a reaction. When you say a command, you plant it in the subconscious mind, and it begins to grow into an action. Remember, the subconscious is looking for patterns. And one or two commands are not a pattern. I'll give you a simple example.

Example 1:

Look at a few of these sentences that I have written. This is an example of a real estate agent using correct language commands. The first thing he/she says to the homeowners when he gets to the house is:

"Usually my customers *do as I say*.... Any way shall we *begin*?"

Now, 95% of the time the home owner's reaction will be to say "Okay!" and start working with the real estate agent. Notice the real estate has used two commands in his/her sentence. 1) Do as I say. 2) Begin.

Example 2:

In a business meeting you could say, "You should work with me, so I can help you get what you want." In this case*Work with me* is the command. Essentially there are three techniques to use when imputing correct language commands into your sentences and these are listed below:

1. Pausing before the command words
2. Going louder on the command words
3. Pausing after the embedded words

What you need to do is become very strong and with your language patterns. This is an important part of influencing the prospective employer. Remember, perception is reality. If they think

32

you have power, you do. If they think you're an imposter, they're correct.

Language Interpretation

Human beings interpret information in a variety of ways and we do this using our bodies. Within the realm of communication humans usually use either sight (the eyes) sound (the ears) or touch (using all the body). Typically, we will have our favorites every human does. For instance, I am a person who interprets information mostly through my eyes; that is to say I like to picture things in my mind. I take information in most easily through the use of images and pictures and videos. Some of us, indeed maybe yourself, will like to receive information by listening, for example listening to an audio CD or MP3 player or the radio. Some like to learn via physically touching something or carrying out some type of manual of physical work to understand how a contraption works (just as in the case of children and Lego building blocks). There is no wrong or right way of learning, but the point is that this effects how we are most readily able to receive information.

This may all seem a bit off the point at the moment, but I shall shortly show you how we can use this information to our advantage during an interview. So my friends, we have established that there are basically 3 ways in which we can learn. To use the appropriate scientific terminology these are Visual (seeing), Auditory (hearing) and Kinetic (feeling). Also, we can easily establish who processes information most readily in which way by observing the use of their language. Various studies have shown that the way you interpret information will be represented with the language you use. Now what exactly do I mean by that? As an example we may meet someone who is explaining a situation and they may say at the end of their sentence to the listener "do you see what I'm saying!". The key indicator in this sentence is the word "see". My friends, as apprentice rapport builders we have just been given some very important information.

We can identify by the subjects use of language that this particular person intakes information primarily through visual means. Remember they used the word 'see'. They are highly likely to be stimulated by pictures, diagrams, film and so on. We may in the same way encounter another person who in the exact same situation will say "do you hear what I'm saying". Again as students of this knowledge we are able to ascertain that this particular person primarily is stimulated by sounds, voices, tones, vibration and such like. Again in a third scenario we may hear from another person "Do you feel what I'm saying, or did that speech touch you?". Again we know this person is kinetic, probably a touchy feely person. Okay, so we have established in a few seconds the primary means of information intake of this person.

So how does this help us within the interview?

Well we know that an important part of the interview is encouraging the interviewer to like us, that is to build rapport and seek his or her level. This of course is not the only factor and but it is highly likely that our interviewer will not hire us if they do not like us. Ok friends, so one way in which we can increase rapport and therefore increase our likeability is to use language that our interviewer will be highly susceptible or responsive to.

Applying the use of correct language

Once we have identified what type of interpretation system our interviewer uses we simply insure that in our language and behavior we mirror that system. So as an example, if our interviewer is visual we should try to use visual language and describe ideas in the form of pictures etc. To simplify this, I have created a table at the end of this chapter for you to use as a reference for these situation and provided examples of phrases and behavior that you can use. Before you go on friends, I know that this information is new to you and to some of you who have never heard this before it may seem farfetched and overkill. However, rest assured that these facts are based on evidence collated by hundreds of studies by highly trained doctors and researchers in the field of mind programming, psychology, hypnosis and relationship building.

Therefore, have no doubt that these techniques work and are effective and will influence your level of success. If on the other hand you believe this to be overkill I can only say that success in any field of endeavor is almost always obtained by people who go the extra mile and do what others are not willing to do or lack the knowledge to do. So have no doubt in your mind as to the importance of this my friends. Please utilize the table at the end of this chapter and practice as often as possible, using it within your conversation. You may also at this stage have identified what type of system that you and your friends and family use and you can practice with them.

Good Luck my friends.

Visual	Auditory	Kinetic
"I see what you are saying..."	"I hear you."	"If it feels right, do it."
"That looks good."	"That rings a bell."	"Get a handle on it."
"That idea isn't clear."	"Listen to yourself."	"Grasp the concepts."
"I went blank."	"Something tells me to be careful."	"A solid understanding."
"Let's cast some light on the subject."	"That idea's been rattling around in my head."	"I'm up against the wall."
"A colourful example..."	"It sounds good to me."	"Change your standpoint."
"Get a new perspective."	"Everything just suddenly clicked."	"You're so insensitive."
"I view it this way..."	"I can really tune in to what you're saying."	"I have a feeling you're right."

Words of Wisdom:

"We must become the change we want to see".

Mahatma Gandhi

CHAPTER 6

Researching the Organization

We just keep on bumping into each other don't we my friends! Welcome to Chapter 6!

Again, I congratulate you on your persistence and determination; you will be rewarded for it in due course, trust me. Each of these chapters is providing you with the tools required to achieve your goal in totality. Each chapter brings us a step closer to the interview stage of the process. But before we engage with the potential employer we need to know who we are dealing with. We must understand the organization we are going to be approaching. As with everything in life, preparation is half the battle. Preparation is paramount and you would do well to remember this simple truth. We must know and understand exactly who it is that we will be presenting ourselves to and we must have an excellent understanding of their business or organization if we hope to gain employment there. There are a number of ways to find out information about the organization which we are about to approach for a job via an interview.

Therefore, in-depth research is the key. Let's have a look at some of the methods that myself and other successful veterans in this area have employed (no pun intended) to Get Hired! There are a number of research methods we can use such as newspapers, industry magazines and your local library. All of the above can and should be used, but for the most up to date information I would definitely try utilizing the internet or as it's sometimes known the World Wide Web. Most organizations and businesses these days will be making the use of a website to market their business. I would suggest that this is one of the best sources of information on the organization you are approaching for employment. If you do not know the website address of the company, then you can usually make use of search engines such as www.bing.com or www.google.com.

Firstly, you will of course need access to the internet and a web browser, but once you have access you can begin. By typing in the company name and a few key words relating to the industry into the search bar you will be guided to the website or to a site related to your search. The website will be likely divided into sections such as homepage, contact, company background or history, people, news, jobs, products. All of these will be useful when researching the company, but I would suggest that the company background, people, products and news sections will be of most use to you. There are three very important points to consider during this process. Firstly, let me suggest to you that every prospective employer will have expected you to do at least some research on the company.

In particular, they will expect you to know what the company does i.e. the products or services that it provides or if it is a government or not-for-profit organization the types of services that it provides to its clients. Secondly, I would suggest that it is a good idea to know who the key players within the organization are, especially who the head of the business is. You may come across a number of titles for describing the head of the business namely the, managing director, financial director, CEO (Chief Executive Officer), CIO (Chief Information Officer), COO (Chief Operations Officer), President. (For a more complete listing of business titles you may refer to chapter 10). All of these titles can be put into the generic category of key decision maker, so do not confused by the particular name or description used.

It may be that the organization you are attempting to gain employment with also has advisors, board members or non-executive directors as they are sometimes called, these are secondary in importance but it always looks good if you are aware of the other members of the board as well. We are focused here on who the important people are and what role they play within the organization and this will increase our knowledge of the company/ organization and how it operates. Thirdly, another area to be aware of is the current news or developments within the company or organization. This will show that you have been keeping up to date and are aware of what is happening currently. It is important because it keeps us abreast of recent developments and shows our interest for the industry and business. As your advisor and guide I want to help you to gain the edge and make no mistake, this is one of the easiest and best ways to do this. So those are the three main areas to be aware of when researching the company on the internet and using their website to gain information, but what other ways are there for us to gain information?

As I mentioned previously, the internet while being the favored option for more up to date information is not the only method and in our quest to be masters it would be pertinent to explore even more avenues if we are to gain the edge. So how else can we gain the advantage in this game? What other ways are there? Well friends, we can gain information from magazines. No not FHM or The National Enquirer, I mean industry magazines, this may take a bit of research but almost every market and business sector will have magazines that everyone in that sector uses to keep abreast of the current developments. If it is a new or emerging market then this maybe more difficult, but there will still be publications, reports and white papers that relate to some aspect of the industry. As an example many people in the computing industry in the UK will read Computing Weekly, incidentally this is available on the internet also in the form of www.computing.com. The same goes for other industries such as Law, Medicine, and Finance etc.

Okay, we have that covered, but what else?

Well there are of course seminars and conferences, now if you really want to impress the employer then this is definitely an area to cover; in addition, this will also give you something to talk about during the interview. So you may want to mention that you recently attended the 'so and so conference in Brussels' or 'Silicon Valley' and how much fun it was and what you found interesting and maybe even educate the prospective employer about it. This will definitely impress them and help us with our goal of getting hired.

What else?

Well my friends, how about the recruitment consultants? this may not be applicable if you are applying to a job without the assistance of an RC, but if you happen to be then why not use this extra leverage and gain some much needed information from the recruitment consultant. They may be able to give you some information about the characters within the organization and also the annual turnover and the main competitors as well. Incidentally, they will also be able to give you a heads up on the gossip which can also be useful and also a talking point within the interview (as long as it is not the sexual appetites of the Managing Director) etc. But they are certainly a good source of information, they will probably be well acquainted with the company and there is no harm in asking.

The Conclusion

In conclusion, the correct mind set to have when becoming involved at this stage is that of a private investigator or freelance researcher. Remember to set your goals up in advance before you embark. Be clear about your aims and then utilize every stratagem you can. You must be fully versed before you enter into interaction with the target company. Having this knowledge in advance will provide you with the confidence you require. By the conclusion of your research you should be 100% confident that you can answer almost any question about the company. Your boldness and competence should be obvious. When you begin to have a conversation with the prospective employer the impression you want to leave is that you are almost are already working for the company.

Almost as if you are an external consultant for the company coming back for a catch-up meeting with your line manager. This will incline the prospective employer towards hiring you as he/she notices that you have an enthusiasm for the organization and how well you would fit in. To consolidate this impression, you will need to incorporate one more factor. In addition to an excellent understanding of the organization you will need to be to slightly visionary. You must be very interested in not only where the company is today but where they are going as well. Understanding the industry, you are in will provide you with an insight as to what the current trends are, but you must be able to identify where the company fits in within the market.

This will impress the prospective employer. This shows that you are not just a person who is able to memorize information and regurgitate it, but also a forward thinker, a visionary. This is very important as no organization or company has the luxury of being able to stand still, but must able to keeping moving with the times if they want to continue being at the cutting edge of their industry. So go forth and become investigators and researchers and reporters for a few days and see what you can dig up. Then compile it and review, read and remember the keys points. Use them within your rehearsals as outlined in the previous chapters and use them within the battle ground that is the interview and I guarantee that you will increase your likelihood of success.

Go for it!

Words of Wisdom:

"In making a speech one must study three points: first, the means of producing persuasion; second, the language; third the proper arrangement of the various parts of the speech."

Aristotle

CHAPTER 7

Unorthodox Interviews and Presentations

Welcome to Chapter 7 my friends, and well done on making it this far. You are making great progress!

Now, I'd like to speak to you about the latter stages of the employment process. It is time to start to focus on the interview and focus on preparation. These days because of the competition for employment roles and the variety of skills required for roles, the interview process has also changed. It is important to know that not all interviews are of the standard type; they vary from organization to organization. Depending on the type of industry you are seeking to join the interview process will undoubtedly change accordingly. We must be prepared for all situations. We need to understand what the different types of interviews are and prepare for them in advance so that we are not caught unaware and unprepared. So what are the possible scenarios that we may come across? There are a number of different interview types and so we will look at each one individually.

The Telephone Interview:

Okay friends, first up we have the telephone interview which is becoming used more frequently within the employment application process. The telephone interview is simply an interview which happens over the telephone rather than face to face. Often these days you will find prospective employers use the telephone interview as a pre-cursor to the real face to face interview. In this way the telephone interview acts as a filtering system that is able to reduce the volume of candidates to those that they deem as most suitable for employment. Unfortunately, we are limited in the number of positions of influence that we have during a telephone interview by the fact that we are in a different location to the interviewer and have no ability to form a visual representation or interact with them in close proximity.

Therefore, dress codes, facial expressions, bodily movements and alike are all null and void within this scenario. We must be able to rely on two main factors. First our level of skill at answering the questions and second our delivery of those answers. When I say 'delivery' what I am alluding to is our ability to convey good telephone manner. In fact, you will find on many job descriptions that this is a skill most employers are looking for, particularly within office, sales and secretarial roles. Often a job description under the requirements section will say 'good telephone manner required'. You will remember from the previous chapters that we said that preparation was a key element of success and we suggested video recording your interview in advance.

Well, I would suggest that this scenario requires the same type of preparation. We must sound clear and articulate over the telephone. Muffled answers, mumbling and excessive speed or lack of speed are all pitfalls to be avoided. It is advisable that you record yourself answering a series of questions and then play it back to yourself taking note of your answers and also how you sound. Remember that it is imperative to practice again and again until you are happy with your level of delivery. Another note to remember is that the interviewer will be able to hear in your voice if you have a smile on your face. It will come across even though they cannot see you and this is where the classic sales rule of 'smile while you dial' comes from.

The Group Activity Interview

Upon careful observation you will soon realize that these day's interactive group interviews are taking place more and more. The idea behind these types of interviews comes from the fact that during your employment you will be working within some type of group or team and consequently the prospective employer would like to see how you function within a group in advance. They will then use the results they receive to ascertain whether or not you are suitable for the position. Again, these types on interview can be difficult and throw you off guard, especially if you were expecting a conventional interview. Remember, the prospective employer may not inform you in advance that you will be participating in a group exercise. The activities may take the form of creating games, discussions or even constructing and organizing company procedures. Just about anything these employers can dream up may be used a test.

The most common form used is usually the creation of a game by a group. You may have to pit your wits against other groups within these exercises. Remember, no matter the activity being used by the employer what they are really looking for is evidence of your interactive skills and social confidence. So let's list some areas which they will be monitoring. Typically, the following attributes or talents will be in demand, leadership skills, organizational skills, pleasant demeanor, rapport building skills, energy, enthusiasm, quick thinking, work under pressure or time limits, creativity, dynamism, reasoning and ability to back up arguments for decisions with evidence, and playfulness. There may be others, but these are usually the main ones and the amount of focus will depend on what position and in which field you are applying for.

Remember you must make a display of your talents otherwise they will never know what you are capable of. You must have no hesitation, but move boldly and enthusiastically display your skills so that they have no doubt of your abilities. But also remember not to play up too much to the observers as this will also be noted, engage 100% in whatever task has been set and remember to have fun.

Spontaneous Interview

I remember some years ago when I was very young, I applied for a job as a waiter within a well-known a Mexican restaurant chain called Chiqitos in Europe. This Mexican restaurant was known for its fun and high energy atmosphere. During the interview group activities were assigned to us as a means of assessment. At one point each one of us candidates were asked to stand up and walk to the front of the room and in front of the other applicants and observers pretend to jump out of an airplane. This was sprung on us spontaneously with no warning whatsoever. The lesson here is that we must be prepared for this type of surprise assessment. This is an example of a spontaneous interview. It may be the case that even within a normal face to face interview you may suddenly be asked to perform some type of action displaying your skills without prior warning.

For example, within sales interviews it is not uncommon for an interviewer to stop midway and identify an object within the room and say "sell this to me". You will then have to switch your state of mind and go into a full blown sales pitch on a lead pencil for example. So again, we have had to practice our abilities to adapt to changing circumstances. We should not be surprised if we are asked to engage in some type of show of our abilities at a moment's notice, indeed we should expect it. Also, it is relatively easy to know in advance what to expect in terms of the request by the type of role we are applying for.

As an example if we were being interviewed for the role of a computer programmer then we should not be surprised if we are asked to write down some code for part of a program on the spot.

Similarly, if we are being interviewed for a sales role then we should expect to have to sell something on the spot. The list goes on and on. Remember here that practice is the key and we must rehearse these scenarios out before the interview, so that we cannot be caught unaware. Remember friends that repetition is the mother of skill.

The Video Conference Interview:

This method is gaining popularity as we are now within the technological age. Sometimes referred to as VOI (video online conferencing), it has been used as a medium of communication within the corporate world for some time now, and of course it would only be a matter of time before it was used within other areas. Hence, now we may find it within the realm of the interview and as time passes and these technologies become cheaper and more widely available we should expect this to increase. So what is the purpose of Video Conferencing Interview? The VOI simply replaces the in person interview, the candidate and employer are able to look at each other and talk with each other in the same room. Some companies have reported to have hired personnel right from video. This form of interview is mostly restricted to office based positions. So there is really not much difference between this and an in-person interview as the employer can see you almost as well as he/she would if he/she were in the same room as you.

I would suggest that if possible you test the equipment you are using beforehand in a trial run to ensure that the connection is good and the picture is clear. However, all of the usual rules of engagement should be employed as if you were in the normal situation, please refer to the previous chapters for clarification of the important elements that make up a successful interview. This should have given you a good overview of some of the different types of interviews you will be faced with. Remember that anticipation and practice will be the cornerstone of success here.

You can now move forward with even more confidence safe in the knowledge that you cannot be caught out by surprise.

As always friends, good luck.

Words of Wisdom:

"Action is the foundational key to all success".

Pablo Picasso

CHAPTER 8

Closing

Welcome back. I'm sure you have been paying very close attention to every chapter, moreover to every word. Remember that planning all the way to the end is an important component of success. Every detail must be prepared for and every aspect must be completed in totality to perfection. This may seem extreme but please understand that success in any area is no mere accident. So, we have looked at every aspect of the employment process so far, from beginning to end, we have looked at the techniques we need to master within the interview. But the end is just as important as the beginning. We cannot simply give a fantastic interview and leave it at that. No, we have to close the interview at the end to secure our position. In the language of the employment and recruitment business this is called a "close".

What it a close?

In simple terms the definition of a close is 'the steps we take to persuade the employer to make the necessary commitment to hiring you'. The close is usually done by putting the prospective employer on the spot at the end of the interview and attempting to extract a positive conformation of a job offer. Shortly, we will look at some principles and examples but first let us look at some must do's for the interview stage. All three must be completed to ensure a successful conclusion to the interview process.

I.   Never leave the interview without knowing what the next stage in the process is (you can find out by simply asking, do not guess),

II. II. Never leave a job interview without communicating clearly the qualifications and the benefits you will bring to the job.

III. III. Never leave the interview without 'opening the door' for a follow up, again you can do this by asking for or informing them that you will be calling shortly for some feedback.

So as we have identified, the close is simply where we attempt to gain the verbal yes from the interviewer or prospective employer within the meeting. This is very important as it again shows our enthusiasm for the role and determination to gain employment within the organization. As well as ensuring that we stand out from our competition (the other candidates), we also ensure that we convey to the prospective employer that they have no reason not to hire us. Now any good employer will certainly expect you to close and if you do not then this is a sure sign that you are either not keen or very inexperienced and we must definitely not give the impression that we are any of these.

How do we close?

Below you can see an example of a simple close:

Example 1:

"Do you see any gaps between my qualifications and experience and the requirements for the job?"

Or even.

Example 2:

"Based on what we have discussed today do you have any concerns about my ability to do this job?"

Let us take note of the previous examples. The aim here with the closes previously provided is to prompt the prospective employer to provide reasons why you may not be correct for the role to use a gambling term "lay his or her cards on the table". Once we have obtained their final concerns then our job is to dispel those concerns one by one and once we have ensured that they are happy with the answers to ask the question again. We want to lightly pressure them with tact into positive response or at least an acknowledgment that you are correct for the role in question. Remember also that we must be ready to answer any concerns they have. We should have already prepared our answers and I have prepared a chapter dealing with possible questions the interviewer may ask so that you will have the resources you need. There is a very simple five step formula for following up your closing statements during the final part of the interview and it is as follows:

1) Sell your qualifications (benefits).
2) Ask for objections
3) Listen Carefully
4) Overcome Objections
5) Re-state your qualifications

Below I have provided you with a closing statement which you can use or modify as you see fit.

Example 1:

"Well as I understand, your position requires (give job description), my qualifications fit this position very well, since it requires (give your matching qualifications). Is that correct?

Example 2:

"There seems to be a good match here. From what you've explained, the job calls for, (give job description) am I right? Then my qualifications seem tailor-made! Don't you think so?

As well as the above example we can ask the employer if we are able to contact them after the interview, this is a variation of the standard close.

I have outlined below 13 different closing techniques which you can select from and use as appropriate.

Thirteen Closing Techniques

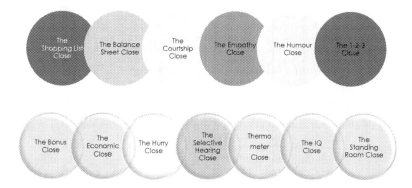

1) The Shopping List Close

Technique

First elicit the interviewer's needs, including requirements of the job role and other elements such as commitment levels, responsibilities and so on. (We can call these 'items' for the purposes of this close). Write these items down and verify with the interviewer that this is what they want. Of course ensure that everything you write down is something that you have the skills and experience to provide. Then show the interviewer the items on the list. The 'shopping list' close is done as you check off each item as you show it. If you can't cover everything, make sure the things you can't cover are (a) few and (b) relatively unimportant.

Examples

"OK. So what you want is a sales executive with 3 or more years' experience, with a solid track record of success. In addition, you would like them to be educated to degree level with some experience of the financial world. Well here is your list. Let's see if we've covered it? 3 years' experience (check), degree educated reduction (check), experience of the financial world (check). That's it. I've got it all. So what do you say?"

How it works

The Shopping List close works by convincing the interviewer that the list itself is all that they need; this is done by careful questioning and writing in a form where you can demonstrate competence. The convincing part of the close is in the way that you check off each item. The effect is that each time you do this; it causes the interviewer to experience a psychological close. The repetition is like a series of hammer blows that create a strong final close. The completed list is also ensures that the interviewer cannot have any objections.

2) The 1-2-3 Close

Technique

Summarize in sets of three items, for example, I will give you this, that and the other. This may be features of your CV/ Resume or some additional benefits that you offer. There are two ways to do this: they may either be closely related (to reinforce a single point) or may be quite separate (to gain greater coverage). This is the classic business measurement trilogy of cost, quality and time.

Examples

"I have the appropriate skills, experience and motivation."

"I can provide the vision, organization and execution required for this role."

How it works

The 1-2-3 Close works through the principle of triples, a pattern where the three areas given together act as a coherent set of three strong points that give a compelling message. (The human mind is typically very receptive to the concept of triple configurations and they are used very often in phrases. Example "sun, sea and sand" or "father, son, holy ghost" or "me, myself and I").

3) The Balance Sheet Close

Technique

This close takes some skill and should be used when only when you are very experienced. You list both the benefits of hiring yourself (the pros) and also the implications or costs (the cons). Of course, the pros (the reasons to hire you) must outweigh the cons. You can even write it down like the balance sheet previously. Make sure the 'pros' column is longer and more impressive, of course. Start with the cons and keep them short. But do make it sound credible, as if you are giving them fair consideration. Then cover the pros. Perhaps sound pleasantly surprised as you describe them. Sound reasonable, as if you are on their side. Sound almost as if you are talking to yourself.

Examples

> "Well, although I'm asking for $75,000 per annum you are getting someone that will require minimum training and can be productive immediately. Let's weigh things up. You're currently not getting as many sales as you could and your business is suffering...it seems to me the cost to your business is greater".

How it works

The Balance Sheet Close works by building trust through appearing to be taking a balanced and fair approach. It guides the other person's thinking and hopefully saves them the trouble of weighing up the pros and the cons. This is also known as the Abraham Lincoln Close (American President Abraham Lincoln was a lawyer and often used this technique in his cases).

4) The Bonus Close

Technique

When they are dithering close to a decision, offer them something unexpected and un-asked for that delights them. A simple equation to illustrate the technique: delight = expectation + 1. Try and figure them out before using this close and be very careful because for some interviewers it will open them up again to more negotiation and they will seek to gain even more.

Examples
1. "You know, I've really enjoyed meeting you and really like the company so I'm prepared to work the first two weeks for no pay to show my commitment."
2. "Don't worry about providing me with sales contacts I am able to bring a database of hot leads once I accept the role."

How it works

The Bonus Close may work in several ways. First, the bonus is a temptation. The interviewer may feel that they have got something for nothing, they may agree to the deal for fear that you may take it away from them again. You may also create a sense of exchange, where because you have given them something they feel obliged to offer you something in return (the job hopefully).

5) The Courtship Close

Technique

Woo the other person like you were wooing a mate. Pay attention to them. Give them sincere compliments. Buy them a coffee, if it is appropriate. Put them on a pedestal. Generally, treat the other person as if you like them, as a person, and that the job is a secondary issue. If the interview process is taking place over a period of time, work hard to develop the relationship. Call them often enough to show your interest. Be someone who makes them feel special. The final request for the job role should be like proposing marriage to them. If they truly love you (or at least how you have been treating them), they will, of course, say yes. Beware of harassment, stalking and other unwanted attention, of course. Be respectful. You want to attract them, not frighten them away.

Examples

You know, you really look professional in that suit, I can see why you are the boss. It's so lovely talking to a person like you...No, it's no bother at all... Let me take that for you...oh, you're witty, too.

How it works

Obtaining employment and the interview itself is very close in many ways to courtship. The Courtship Close works by using many of the methods that young men use to seduce young women. So know the triggers and press the right buttons and the other person will be flattered enough to buy you, hook, line and sinker.

6) The Economic Close

Technique

Focus on the overall economics of hiring you, showing how the cost is less by considering certain factors. Show how employing you will provide an excellent return on investment and the financial rewards or cost reductions you will bring to the organization. Show how alternatives have hidden costs. Talk about the longer-term costs of alternatives and long term benefits of hiring you.

Examples:

"...Yes, it is cheaper to hire someone of less experience but will they be able to deliver for the firm in the way that I can? Can I ask what you believe to be the opportunity cost of not hiring me? What I can do and deliver, will mean that your investment in me will generate x, now let's look at the number and my track record of delivering on my promises..."

How it works

Many employers focus solely on cost, and this close plays directly to their concerns by showing you are trying to save them money. By doing this, you also gain trust. Even those who are not so concerned about price will have it as an issue at some level, and again you will impress them by taking up this cause for them.

7) Empathy Close

Technique

Empathize with the interviewer and try to understand what they feel. Walk a mile in their shoes. Attempt to understand their situation completely. Act like you are helping them out. Be a match-maker in bringing yourself and skills to a worthy organization.

Examples:

"...I completely understand...and it makes so much sense to me now. I really can appreciate your situation and why you need to fill this position...".

How it works

The Empathy Close works by first harmonizing yourself with the employer and then, when you feel what it is like for them and they believe that you do, they will naturally come along with you. Done well, you will close at exactly the right moment and for exactly the right reasons for them. The Empathy Close is also called the Love Close.

8) The Embarrassment Close

Technique

Maneuver them into a position where not hiring you would embarrass them. Dissuade them from hiring other people or choosing another option by pointing out that they are not worthy of the firm, low in ability or effectiveness, not as good value as you etc. and that you are a better and of greater value. Tell stories of cheapskates who make 'false savings with the cheap options. Sell yourself to the people they are with, so the other person would have to disappoint superiors in the firm by not making the correct choice. Appeal to their sense of self-importance and affluence.

Examples:

1. "..This is the other option. I am the best choice however and of more value to your firm because............."
2. "...Well, it looks like your colleagues agree with me..."
3. "....Not many employers would have the vision to see the benefit here but I can see that you can....."

How it works

The Embarrassment Close appeals to human emotions such as pride. It uses an alignment principle to get people to align their actions with their self-image of kindness and affluence, etc.

It works particularly well if the interviewer is with others where the embarrassment would be particularly strong, from a group of peers or colleagues or superiors.

Young and ambitious men, perhaps unsurprisingly, are particularly susceptible to the Embarrassment Close.

9) The Hurry Close

Technique

Hurry them up with regard to their decision on hiring you. Speed up the proceedings. Talk fast, move fast. Encourage them to do the same. Hint that slower thinking is not very clever. Say that if they cannot decide quickly then others employers might hire you and they miss out.

Examples

1. "............Yes sir, this is the best way forward let's get this moving, how soon can I sign a contract...let's do something today...."
2. "............If you want to succeed then you must speed, or others will get there first, I have a company I need to give an answer to in the next 2 hours.........".

How it works

Speeding employer's up stops them from pausing to think about reasons why they should not hire you.

10) The IQ Close

Technique

Imply that intelligent people would hire you immediately. The intelligence can also be associated just with doing a good business deal for the organization. You can also imply that it is stupid not to hire you.

Examples

1. "The person who hired me was a man of great intelligence, a very successful businessman".
2. "It's a bit complex to understand all the benefits I bring to your firm, but you look like you can handle it..........".

How it works

The IQ Close works by associating intelligence with closure. Thus, if people think they are intelligent (and we all do) they will be attracted towards hiring you and hence feeling that they are intelligent. If the person has an avoidance preference, then implying they would be stupid not to buy makes them aim to avoid the stupidity.

11) The Selective Hearing Close

Technique

Also known as the Selective-Deafness close, you ignore anything that the other person says or does that does not lead you towards a close in your favor. Think hard about what they are saying and seek ways to lead them away from it. This must be done with lots of tact.

Examples:

1. The employer say's it is too expensive: — "..........Won't it be great when we are able to start bringing in new business?".
2. They ask about things you do not have: — "......One of the great things about me is that I am a very fast learner?"

How it works

The Selective-Deafness Close works by the principle that you get what you talk about. If their attention is on why they cannot hire you, then they are likely to not hire you. It also is related to the locus of control. If you are talking about what they want, you are on their agenda and they are in control. What you want is for them to think that they are in control, but they are actually walking down the path you control.

12) The Standing Room Only Close

Technique

Show how other people are all queuing up to hire you. Indicate that they need to move quickly. Hint that they may be left behind by others. Remember you need to be tactful.

Examples

1. "...I have had six interviews this week yesterday and every one of them have given me a job offers. If I were you I'd make you offer now. I'd get my application in quick......"
2. ".........I don't know how many more interviews I'll really need to do; I may not need to do any......"

How it works

The Standing-room-only lose works by the evidence principle, where the evidence of other people's interest in you is available and you socialize it. It works best therefore if you can prove in some way that you have offers, if you can at least show one, you can always be creative with the truth about the other five or so. It shows that the employer is not an early adopter but runs the danger of being in the late majority or even seen as a laggard, slow and not up to speed when it comes to employing you.

13) The Thermometer Close

The thermometer close is what I would call an upfront closing technique, by using the technique you are not trying to close the sale out but merely attempting to move the conversation and the employment opportunity forward.

It goes like so:

You: Hi, this is (your name). How are you today?

Next the stall:

Prospect: Oh Hi (Salesperson) I'm good, unfortunately we are not going to make a decision on your application yet so perhaps if you could leave it till next week that would be great. Here comes the upfront closing technique, which allows you to test where the employment is relative to a successful close.

You: No problem, I will put you down for a call on Tuesday. Obviously I would like it be a yes on Tuesday but if was to ask you say on a scale of one to ten, ten being we definitely will be doing business and one being we definitely won't be doing business, where would you say you are right now?

Employer: Oh I say a seven or eight.

Depending on the number, you know how much convincing is left to do. An Answer of five or less means lots and an answer of six or more means not so much. The Thirteen Closing techniques need to be practiced in advance of the interview. This will ensure that they are firmly conditioned into your mind and you will be able to draw upon them at the appropriate time. It is also possible to use a combination of the closing techniques, as example you may want to warm up the interviewer with the The Bonus Close and then finish them off with the Shopping List Close.

However, two closing techniques should be the maximum. While our aim is to gain a positive conclusion and commitment to being hired within the interview if they refuse we need to be able to respect their decision. Many employers will be looking out to see if you try and close them as this is a sign of experience and desire for the position. I hope this has been useful and remember that practice makes perfect.

Good luck guys! You can do it!

Words of Wisdom:

> *"Winners are men who have dedicated their whole lives to winning."*

Woody Hayes

CHAPTER 9

Following Up

Welcome to Chapter 9, you have done extremely well to come this far and I applaud your tenacity and determination. It says a lot about how serious and committed you are, so keep going. So, the interview is now over and we can just relax and wait for the result confident in the knowledge that we have given it our best shot. After all, we have utilized everything we have learnt in these pages so far and success is now virtually guaranteed at this point.

No! ... Incorrect my friends!

If we are to be totality successful we must see our plan all the way through to the end. I really want to impress this upon you because it is so important and a factor which too many people miss. It is the first step on the road to failure. I do not intend to let you fail! First of all, let us start by looking at what some of the wise men of our age have said about this.

Napoleon Bonaparte

"If you start to take Vienna, take Vienna".

Joe Namath

"If you aren't going all the way, why go at all?".

John Calvin

"You must submit to supreme suffering in order to discover the joy of completion".

Admiral John Fisher

"Moderation in war is imbecility".

Dear reader I hope you understand that winning is in the execution, that is to say we plan all the way to the end and we take action all the way to the end. As mentioned before, we may have reached the interview stage and completed it. We may have also closed or at least tried to. But we do not stop there, we must follow up. We of course are assuming at this stage that we have not received a verbal yes from the interviewer.

After the interview it may be the case that you have been told that 'you will be contacted' if you have been successful or that simply that 'they will be in contact with us', this is common. However, we must be determined to be successful and get hired and as a consequence we must be proactive. It is therefore imperative that we do not lose under any circumstances, our zeal and determination. It is up to us to prove that we are eager to move ahead and so we must "follow up".

What does it mean to follow up?

To follow up with a prospective employer simply means to re-contact them and ask about the current status of our application. It is also an opportunity for us to re-state our enthusiasm for the employment position and also to remind the prospective employer of our skills and experience. This can take place either post-interview or pre- 2nd interview. Job positions have been won and lost simply on which candidate bothered to follow up and close the employer down on a positive decision. If you have been in direct contact with the employer then of course you can approach them directly, otherwise you may need to make contact via other people.

You may have been utilizing the services of a recruitment consultant. In this case you will need to contact them as they are acting on your behalf; however, if you find them un-responsive or not proactive enough then you can circumvent the consultant and contact the prospective employer directly. Remember that the prospective employer will likely be paying the recruitment consultant from 5-20% of your annual wage as a finder's fee. If they are able to avoid paying the fee by hiring you directly they may be more eager to arrange this. The recruitment consultant may not be overjoyed that you have decided to cut him or her out of the deal at them last minute. But sometimes the ends justify the means.

Follow Up Tips

Remember that we must always make time to follow-up all of our job leads, no matter how busy you are. An application to a job role is not complete until you have followed up after the interview; it is not an optional extra. Follow-up in a timely fashion usually a week to 10 days for conventional job-searching, and even sooner for online applications. Create a job leads spreadsheet so that you have a record of your job-search and follow-ups. If you apply online for a position, consider following-up the online application with a cover letter and resume/CV sent to the employer via postal mail. This will allow you to stand out from the other online applicants because few will also send a hard copy. The idea of the follow up is also to give us the edge over our competition.

Try to keep your follow-up brief, to the point, and professional. You may want to focus your follow-up on why you are a good fit for the position and organization and your 'unique selling points' (USP's). You might also ask the employer if he/she needs any further information not included in your original application. This enables you to continue the conversation, build more rapport and keep yourself in the mind of the prospective employer. If you have recently completed some training, received an award, or earned some other recognition that would make you an even better candidate for the position, be sure to mention it in your follow-up just in case they have forgotten. Continue following-up regularly, but don't overdo it. You need to be keen, but not a stalker.

Structure of the Follow-Up:

There are three key methods of follow up: (a) Letter (b) Email (c) Telephone Call.

A) The Letter Follow Up

1. Express Your Enthusiasm: Convey your interest in and enthusiasm for the company and the position for which you were interviewed. Try to be specific about why you are interested in the position and why you are a good fit for the team and company.

2. Address Unresolved Points: Address any issues or questions that came up during the interview that you feel you did not fully answer. This letter is your last chance to make a positive impression on the interviewer so use it effectively.

3. Personalize It: You will likely be one of many interviewee's, so you need to set yourself apart from the other candidates so they will remember you. In your letter, highlight key points from your interview that you believe the interviewer will remember, this will help them to recall you more easily. Additionally, if you meet with more than one person, consider sending them all thank you letters, each one a bit different; as you may not know exactly who in the group will be making the decisions. Acquiring a business card from each interviewer will help you with names and titles when you sit down to write your thank you letters.

4. Reiterate Your Expertise: If the company has communicated clearly its specific needs, issues or

challenges, use your thank-you letter to demonstrate how you can meet those needs.

5. Highlight Your Successes: Similarly, if the company communicated its ideal qualifications for a candidate, use your thank-you letter to outline how you meet or exceed those qualification requirements.

6. Proofread, and then Proofread again: Make sure your thank you letter conveys a professional image by ensuring it is free of typos and grammatical errors.

B) The Email Follow Up

Always address your email to your contact at the prospective employer; this could be one of the directors or heads of department. Keep your email short and to the point. Simply again state your interest in the job and your key qualifications for it. Be sure to spell-check and proofread your e-mail before sending it. Remember to check your email regularly. Now, because e-mail is such a one-way communication, and you don't really know if your e-mail is even being read, consider asking for a phone number so you can then follow-up by phone (And if you get no response, do your research and uncover the phone number).

C) The Telephone Follow Up

The email, letter and telephone call are fairly similar and the only difference is the vehicle of delivery rather than the content. With regard to telephone follow up there are a few goals which we are aiming for. Firstly, remember that during the interview itself we must thank the prospective employers for their time, and then secondly we must present again the benefits of hiring us and convey that we expect to speak verbally with them soon and anticipate a favorable response. Remember friends, human beings typically get what they expect and more of what they focus on. Below I have constructed an example telephone call.

The key steps in the telephone call are as follows:

- Sit down with a notepad and pen about a week after the job interview to make the follow-up call. Having a notepad on hand will help you take any notes that come up on your follow-up call.
- Call the place where you interviewed and ask to speak to the person you interviewed with.
- Tell the interviewer your name, why you are calling and remind him/her when you had the interview. This will refresh their mind as to whom they are speaking with.
- Ask the interviewer about the status of the position you interviewed for. If the position is still open, ask if you are still being considered.
- End the follow-up call after your job interview by telling the interviewer that you are still interested in the job and you look forward to hearing from them in the future.

Next I will provide you with some practical examples of how you can implement the techniques above, remember that these are only supposed to be used as guides and you should be adapting each one to your particular situation.

Example Letter

You will find an example of a follow up letter below. This will provide you with the basic structure that you require. Notice how I have used flattery within the initial opening paragraph and then moved to re-iterating my skills. I have also quoted industry magazines to show that I'm up to date and informed, these are all techniques that you can also employ to give you the edge.

1377 North Circle Drive, Toronto, Canada, 44567

Tel: 001-514-393-4567

Email: jean.remy@gmail.com

URL: www.canadianconstruction.com/jeanremy

7th October 2017

Mr. Tahir Suleiman, Vice President DAL Property Group,
800, boulevard De Maisonneuve Est,
Montréal (Québec)
H2L 4L8 Canada

Dear Mr. Suleiman,

Thank you for the opportunity to interview for the commercial project manager position. I am appreciative of the time that you took to introduce me to all of the staff at the Montreal office. During our meeting I told you about my extensive international project management experience. Although our conversation focused on the new Eden Towers project in Khartoum, Sudan, I wanted to return again to our mutual priorities.

During my career as a project manager within the construction industry I have always aimed at delivering high quality projects completed on time and within budget. Most of all I have always ensured that I over delivered in terms of the attention to detail. It is my belief that if I am if a piece of work cannot be completed to a standard then it is not worth doing. Evidence of this can be seen Genesis Fields project I worked on in Shanghai, China last year and the Green Water Shopping Center in Paris, France in 2012 as outlined in my portfolio.

High standards are central to my work and I am therefore compelled to join DAL Property Group as I have paid close attention to your work over the years and notice we share the same obsession for completing high quality construction projects that make a real impact in people's lives.

Thanks again for the interview. I look forward to contacting you next week to check on the progress of my application.

Yours Sincerely,

Jean Remy

Below you will find an example of an email follow up. Notice that the email is short and to the point, typically email follow ups are not as lengthy as the letter version and employers expect them to be short also. It is likely that they receive many more emails than letters and we need to bear this in mind.

Example Email

Dear Mr./Ms. Jones:

On January 23 I submitted a cover letter and resume to apply for the position of general accounts executive at Capricorn Enterprises, Inc. I appreciate the fact that you have many applications to read. However, I am committed to showing you that I am well qualified to fill this opening. Would you have 30 minutes available for an interview this week or next? You can choose the date and time, and I'll be there prepared to talk and listen. Thank you for taking the time to read my request. I look forward to hearing from you and meeting you in person.

Joe Job Seeker (joejobseeker@xyz.com)

Example Follow Up Telephone Call To Resume Application

One way to say this would be:

"Hello, Mr. Ryan, my name is Sara Smith, and I'm a junior biochemistry major at the University of Missouri-Columbia. I'm inquiring about your internship in the environmental safety/compliance department and confirming that you received the resume I sent last week. Have I reached you at a convenient time?"

If you have reached Mr. Ryan at an inconvenient time, be brief and offer to call back later. Once Mr. Ryan indicates that he has received your resume and that it is a good time to talk, you might offer:

"I'm excited about the environmental field, particularly as it pertains to industry. Would it be possible to set up a time to interview and talk further about opportunities in the field?"

Now, if Mr. Ryan is not the appropriate person to speak with, he will most likely forward you to the correct individual. Make sure you ask this individual if she or he would like you to submit additional information. (Somewhere during the conversation, you should mention whether you would like to do the internship for credit or not. This might be important information for some companies.) You may be able to set up an interview; however, be prepared for a couple of other scenarios as well. Your contact might indicate that they are still in the screening process and not prepared to set up interviews. In this case it would be perfectly appropriate to inquire:

"When do you expect to make the decision?"

You may call back if you haven't received notification shortly after the deadline you were given. I hope this chapter has clarified how to follow up on your employment applications, remember that once we learn to follow up on all of our applications it will become a habit and it is an excellent and necessary habit to install in our process. Good Luck! You can do it!

Words of Wisdom:

"Knowledge without action is vanity and action without knowledge is insanity"

Ghazali

CHAPTER 10

Key Business Phrases

One of the best ways to build rapport with a prospective employer is to speak with the same language. In general, within the business world we come across language and words which may be at times new to us. As with all aspects of the application process we must be prepared. We will come across business phrases and we will need to know the specific words, phrases and their meanings also. Below I have compiled for you a list of business and office work place terminology that you are likely to come across. Learn each word and their meanings; understand how they are applied by expanding your research of each word. Using the internet will help you to construct a greater understanding. The words and terminology are in alphabetical order. Now my friends, this may seem like a time consuming activity and it is, however the increased confidence that you will feel as a result will increase your chances of success. You will not be surprised or caught out by any terminology that may be thrown at you within the interview or any competency tests. This exercise is essential so do it with conviction, good luck.

Accounts Payable—short term debts incurred as the result of day-to-day operations.

Accounts Receivable—monies due your enterprise as the result of day-today operations.

Assets—all real or intellectual property owned by the enterprise that has a positive financial value.

Accounting—The recording, classifying, summarizing and interpreting in a significant manner and in terms of money, transactions and events of a financial character.

AMEX (American Stock Exchange)—The second-largest stock exchange in the United States. It trades mostly in small-to medium-sized companies.

Annual Percentage Rate (APR)—The periodic rate times the number of periods in a year. For example, a 5% quarterly return has an APR of 20%

Annual Report—Yearly record of a publicly held company's financial condition. It includes a description of the firm's operations, its balance sheet and income statement. SEC rules require that it be distributed to all shareholders. A more detailed version is called a 10-K.

Asset—Any possession that has value in an exchange.

Average Rate of Return (ARR)—The ratio of the average cash inflow to the amount invested. Acquisition—The acquiring of products, assets or services with appropriated funds through purchase or lease.

Affiliates—Business concerns, organizations, or individuals that control each other or that are controlled by a third party. Control may include shared management or ownership; common use of facilities, equipment, and employees; or family interest.

Amortization—Reduction of debt through installed payments.

Appreciation—The increase in value of an asset.

Assets—Cash, property and other resources owned by a firm or person.

Auction—A public sale of goods to the highest bidder.

Authorized Stock—The number of shares of stock that a corporation is permitted to issue. This number of shares is stipulated in the corporation's— state-approved charter, and may be changed by a vote of the corporation's stock-holders.

Balance Sheet—A report of a corporation's financial condition at a specific time.

Bankruptcy—A condition in which a business cannot meet its debt obligations and petitions a federal district court for either reorganization of its debts or liquidation of its assets. In the action the property of a debtor is taken over by a receiver or trustee.

Balance Sheet—a statement of assets and liabilities.

Barriers to Entry—conditions that create difficulty for competitors to enter the market. For example, copyrights, trademarks, patents, dedicated distribution channels and high initial investment requirements.

Bear Market—Any market in which prices are in a declining trend.

Blue-chip Company—Large and creditworthy company.

Break-Even analysis—An analysis of the level of sales at which a project would make zero profit.

Break-Even Point—The point at which revenues are equal to expenses.

Board of Directors—Individuals elected by stockholders to establish corporate management policies. A board of directors decides, among other issues, if and when dividends will be paid to stockholders.

B2B = Business to Business

B2C = Business to Customer

Business Plan—A comprehensive planning document which clearly describes the business developmental objective of an existing or proposed business. The plan outlines what and how and from where the resources needed

Capital—the financial investment required to initiate and/or operate an enterprise.

Capital Expenditures -Amount used during a particular period to acquire or improve long-term assets such as property, plant or equipment.

Consolidation—The combining of two or more firms to form an entirely new entity.

Credit Risk—The risk that an issuer of debt securities or a borrower may default on his obligations.

Change Management - is a structured approach to change in individuals, teams, organizations and societies that enables the transition from a current state to a desired future state.

Cash Flow—The transfer of monies into and out of an enterprise.

Collateral—Assets that can be pledged to guarantee a loan.

Cost of Sales—The cost of goods plus the expenses involved in selling and delivering the product or service.

Current Assets—Assets that can be converted quickly to cash.

Current Liabilities—All debts incurred in the normal day-to-day business and due within one calendar year.

CEO—Chief Executive Officer Description: is the highest-ranking corporate officer (executive) or administrator in charge of total management of an organization. An individual appointed as CEO of a corporation, company, organization, or agency reports to the board of directors.

CIO—Chief Information Officer Description: The chief information officer (CIO), or information technology (IT) director, is a job title commonly given to the most senior executive in an enterprise responsible for the information technology and computer systems that support enterprise goals. The CIO typically reports to the chief executive officer, chief operations officer or chief financial officer. In military organizations, they report to the commanding officer.

Capital—Assets less liabilities, representing the ownership interest in a business; a stock of accumulated goods, especially at a specified time and in contrast to income received during a specified time period; accumulated goods devoted to the product.

Capital Gain—The profit realized when a capital asset is sold for a higher price than the purchase price. See also capital loss.

Capital Loss—The loss incurred when a capital asset is sold for a lower price than the purchase price. See also capital gain.

Cash Flow—An accounting presentation showing how much of the cash generated by the business remains after both expenses (including interest) and principal repayment on financing are paid. A projected cash flow statement indicates whether the business will have cash.

Collateral—Something of value—securities, evidence of deposit or other property—pledged to support the repayment of an obligation.

Collateral Document—A legal document covering the item(s) pledged as collateral on a loan, i.e., note, mortgages, assignment, etc.

Consortium—A coalition of organizations, such as banks and corporations, set up to fund ventures requiring large capital resources.

Contract—A mutually binding legal relationship obligating the seller to furnish supplies or services and the buyer to pay for them.

Costs—Money obligated for goods and services received during a given period of time.

Debt—Money borrowed and owed.

Debt Financing—The provision of long term loans to small business concerns in exchange for debt securities or a note.

Depreciation—The gradual erosion of the usability and value (possibly due to obsolescence) of an enterprise's fixed assets. In some cases, depreciation can be declared as a tax deduction.

Distributor—an enterprise that purchases your products for resale to their customers who are sometimes retail outlets. The distributor expects to receive a significant price discount for providing the distribution service.

Distribution Channel—the path your product follows to be delivered to the end user. This may be through distributors, retail outlets, self service outlets, vending machines, telephone sales, direct mail sales, etc.

Deferred Loan—Loans whose principal and or interest installments are postponed for a specified period of time.

Dividend—A distribution of the earnings of a corporation. Dividends may be in the form of cash, stock or property. All dividends must be declared by the board of directors

Due Diligence—The careful investigation by the underwriters that is necessary to ensure that all material information pertinent to an issue has been disclosed to prospective investors.

Employment Taxes—federal income tax withholding, social security and Medicare taxes, and federal unemployment tax.

Enterprise—Aggregation of all establishments owned by a parent company. An enterprise can consist of a single, independent establishment or it can include subsidiaries or other branch establishments under the same ownership and control.

Entrepreneur—One who assumes the financial risk of the initiation, operation and management of a given business or undertaking.

Equity—An accounting term used to describe the net investment of owners or stockholders in a business. Under the accounting equation, equity also represents the result of assets less liabilities.

Escrow Accounts—Funds placed in trust with a third party, by a borrower for a specific purpose and to be delivered to the borrower only upon the fulfillment of certain conditions.

Expenses—costs incurred (other than purchases) to carry on a business.

Equity—a percentage ownership of an enterprise, usually in the form of stock.

Fixed Costs—The day-to-day cost of doing business that is pre-committed, such as salaries, insurance, lease expenses, utilities, etc.

Financial Reports—Reports commonly required from applicants request for financial assistance, e.g. Balance Sheet—A report of the status of a firm's assets, liabilities and owner's equity at a given time. Income Statement—A report of revenue and expenses.

Fiscal Tax Year—12 consecutive months ending on the last day of any month other than December, or a 52-53 week year.

Foreclosure—The act by the mortgagee or trustee upon default, in the payment of interest or principal of a mortgage of enforcing payment of the debt by selling the underlying security.

Franchising—A continuing relationship in which the franchisor provides a licensed privilege to the franchisee to do business, and offers assistance in organizing, training, merchandising, marketing and managing in return for a consideration.

Gross Domestic Product (GDP)—The most comprehensive single measure of aggregate economic output. GDP represents the market value of the total output of the goods and services produced by a nation's economy.

Gross National Product (GNP)—A measure of a nation's aggregate economic output. Since 1991 GDP, a slightly different calculation, has replaced GNP as a measure of U.S. economic output.

Guaranteed Loan—A loan made and serviced by a lending institution under agreement that a governmental agency will purchase the guaranteed portion if the borrower defaults.

Insolvency—The inability of a borrower to meet financial obligations as they mature, or having insufficient assets to pay legal debts.

Interest—An amount paid a lender for the use of funds.

Income Statement— (sometimes called Profit & Loss statement) a statement of revenues and expenses.

Intangible Assets—non-physical assets such as patents, trademarks, a customer base, brand recognition of your products, etc. This is sometimes called goodwill.

Investment Banking—Businesses specializing in the formation of capital. This is done by outright purchase and sale of securities offered by the issuer, standby underwriting or "best efforts selling."

Invitation for Bids—Formal solicitations for offerings, to perform procurements by competitive bids when the specifications describe the requirements of the government clearly, accurately, and completely; but avoiding unnecessarily restrictive specifications or requirements.

Job Description—A written statement listing the elements of a particular job or occupation, e.g., purpose, duties, equipment used, qualifications, training, physical and mental demands, working conditions, etc.

Joint Venture—The cooperation of two or more individuals or enterprises in a specific business enterprise, rather than in continuing relationships as in a partnership.

Liability—A legal obligation to pay a debt owed. Current liabilities are debts payable within twelve months. Long-term liabilities are debts payable over a period of more than twelve months.

Gross Profit—revenues less cost of sales.

Licensing Agreement—an agreement between two enterprises allowing one to sell the other's products or services and to use their name, sales literature, trademarks, copyrights, etc. in a limited manner.

Liquidity—the percentage of an enterprise's assets that can be quickly converted into cash.

Long Term Assets— (sometimes called fixed assets) these are usually non-liquid assets that are integral to the enterprise's day to day business operations such as plants, equipment, furniture and real estate.

Long Term Liabilities—all debts that are not current liabilities, that is, debts that is not due until at least one calendar year in the future.

Limited Partnership (LP)—An association of two or more partners formed to conduct a business jointly and in which one or more of the partners is liable only to the extent of the amount of money they have invested.

Line-of-credit—A lender agrees to allow a borrower to draw a pre-specified amount from an account on an as needed basis.

Liquidation—The disposal, at maximum prices, of the collateral securing a loan, and the voluntary and enforced collection of the remaining loan balance from the obligators and/or guarantors.

Litigation—The practice of taking legal action through the judicial process.

Loan Agreement—Agreement to be executed by borrower, containing pertinent terms, conditions, covenants and restrictions.

Loss Rate—A rate developed by comparing the ratio of total loans charged off to the total loans disbursed from inception of the program to the present date.

Merger—A combination of two or more corporations wherein the dominant unit absorbs the passive ones, the former continuing operation usually under the same name. In a consolidation two units combine and are succeeded by a new corporation, usually with a new title.

Mortgage—An instrument giving legal title to secure the repayment of a loan made by the mortgagee (lender):

Market Life Cycle—the period of time that a substantial segment of the buying public is interested in purchasing a given product or service form.

Market Penetration Pricing Strategy—if near term income is not critical and rapid market penetration for eventual market control is desired, and then you set your prices very low.

Market Share—the percentage of the total sales (from all sources) of a service or product represented by the sales made by your enterprise. i.e. your sales divided by total sales

Net Profit—total revenues less total expenses.

Net Worth—Property owned (assets), minus debts and obligations owed (liabilities), is the owner's equity (net worth).

Ordinary Interest—Simple interest based on a year of 360 days, contrasting with exact interest having a base year of 365 days.

Partnership—a legal relationship between two or more individuals to conduct a specifically defined business.

Profit Margin—total revenues less total expenses

RFP—Request for Proposals

ROI—Return on Investment. The amount of profit (return) based on the amount of resources (funds) used to produce it. Also, the ability of a given investment to earn a return for its use

Return On Equity—A measure of a corporation's profitability, specifically its return on assets, calculated by dividing after-tax income by tangible assets.

Small Business—A business smaller than a given size as measured by its employment, business receipts, or business assets.

Start-up Costs—expenses incurred before the business opens.

Subcontract—A contract between a prime contractor and a subcontractor to furnish supplies or services for the performance of a prime contract or subcontract.

Supporting Documents—information needed to record in one's books, generated from business transactions. These include sales slips, paid bills, invoices, receipts, deposit slips, and cancelled checks.

Turnover (Business)—The amount of money taken by a business in a particular period.

Variable Costs—costs that change as production changes, for example, raw materials, production labor, storage and shipping, etc.

Venture Capital—Money used to support new or unusual commercial undertakings; equity, risk or speculative capital. This funding is provided to new or existing firms that exhibit above-average growth rates, a significant potential for market expansion and the need for add

Working Capital—the cash available to an enterprise for day-to-day operations.

Words of Wisdom:

"Intelligence without ambition is a bird without wings"

Salvador Dali

CHAPTER 11

The After-Interview Checklist

So, how do we become masters? What is it that masters do differently from the rest of us?

I shall tell you.........Masters learn from every mistake that they make. They improve and are able to use the lessons that they have learnt from past failures the next time around. This way they become better and better and eventually masterful. Repeating this process again and again. They also differ their approach when they are not successful with one method. Eventually by using these techniques they become masters. This is what we shall do also; we shall evaluate ourselves after our interview and take note so that we can improve for the next time. Below I have constructed a checklist this just this purpose, after every interview answer the questions below and review your performance.

1. Did you use storytelling, examples, results and measurements of achievements to back up your claims and convince the questioner that you have the skills to do the job?
2. Was your personal grooming immaculate? Were you dressed like company employees?
3. Did you forget any important selling points that you can put in follow-email letter or call back?
4. Did you smile? Did you make eye contact?
5. Did you convey at least five major qualities the interviewer should remember about you?
6. Did you find out the next step and leave the door open for your follow-up?

7. After the interview, did you write down names and points discussed?
8. Did you display high energy? Flexibility? Interest in learning new things?
9. Did the opening of the interview go smoothly?
10. Did you frequently make a strong connection between the job's recruitments and your qualifications?
11. Did you show your understanding of the strategies required to reach company goals?
12. Did you use enthusiasm and motivation to indicate that you're willing to the company?
13. Did you take the interviewer's clues to wrap it up?

Once you have answered these questions remember to highlight any areas you need to improve upon and work on those areas.

Words of Wisdom:

"If you don't take chances, you'll never have the answers"

Nasir Jones

CHAPTER 12

Resume and Covering Letters

An important part of the application process is submitting a resume and covering letter. Below you will see examples of covering letters and also two examples of Resumes / Curriculum Vitae. In the example below let us notice the structure of the covering letter. The applicant has immediately within the first sentence stated which position he/she is applying for; this is important as it avoids confusion. Next the applicant immediately launches into an overview of why he/she is the suitable based on their experience. Remember within these opening lines we only need to briefly give an overview or general idea then we move into details a little later. Notice the second paragraph after goes into more specific details about exactly the kind of experience that the applicant has. The third paragraph now exposes the personality, attributes and benefits of the persona of the applicant. A polite finish inviting the employer to explore the applicants resume / CV and encouraging further contact to be initiated finishes off the letter.

Cover Letter: Example 1

Dear Sir / Madame,

I am writing to express my interest in your current opening for an IT Field Sales Executive therefore, please allow me to submit my curriculum vitae for your review. Having served in an IT Sales and Account Management capacity for almost four years I believe that I have the relevant experience necessary to perform at a high level within the position.

My solution sales and account management experience means I am comfortable presenting and negotiating at director level, constructing proposals, identifying challenges and resolving issues. I am driven to succeed and have been consistently promoted within my current organization.

What I will bring to the position is a combination of enthusiasm, confidence, negotiation skills, and business development skills that I have leveraged to meet and exceed expectations.

In previous positions, I increased sales performance and exceeded targets, because my success in these areas covers multiple environments and businesses, I am confident I will do the same as a member of your team.

My curriculum vitae contain additional details regarding my career accomplishments. I would welcome an opportunity for a personal interview to discuss your organization's needs and the results you can expect from me in addressing those needs. And I thank you in advance for your time and review of my qualifications and experience.

Yours Sincerely,

Cover Letter: Example 2

Date: Thurs, 26 November 2017
From: Jack Frescott (jfrescott@gmail.com)
Subject: Senior Human Resources consultant position at Neptune Investments
To: Adam Smith Attachments: Jack Fresco Resume

Dear Mr Smith,

Having seen your advertisement on www.monster.com and researching your company I would like to apply for the position of Human Resources Consultant. Please find attached my resume for the position of Human Resources Consultant. Currently, I am a Human Resources Manager at Recruit Power. During my 7 years at this company I have hired over 1,000 applicants for positions in dozens of departments, at levels ranging from interns to C-level executives. My experience in handling thousands of candidates will allow me to successfully recruit and manage applicants for your growing company. You will notice from my resume that I also have obtained numerous industry qualification specific to human resources.

Due to my knowledge and experience I feel that I am well qualified to make an effective and useful contribution Neptune Investments recruitment operations. I am enthusiastic about the chance to participate in a meaningful role with an industry leader like Neptune Investments. I look forward to meeting with you to discuss how I may be able to contribute to your organization. Thank you for your consideration of my application.

Please contact me should you require any further information.

Kind Regards,

Jack Frescott

Covering Letter: Example 3:

Samuel Nash 56 Paterson Street,
New Brunswick, New Jersey,
NJ 08903-0964 United States
snash@gmail.com Tel: 001-973-549-6600

Attention: Mr. William Chan Human Resources Manager Graphic
Write 55 East 52nd Street, New York, NY 10722

Dear Mr. Chan,

Your advertisement for a Junior Graphic Designer at Graphic Write has sparked my interest. I have just completed a BSc in Digital Design at Westwood School of Graphic Art in New Jersey. I have provided my resume for your perusal. Currently, I am looking for an entry level position with a reputable industry leader such as Graphic Write. I have been interested in your organization for a number of years and regularly read your blogs and new stories. Over the years I have come to respect the dedication to excellence that you company regularly demonstrates with its work.

During my degree I studied subjects such as Advanced Typography, Color and Surface Design, Web Design, Digital Illustration and Animation. I thoroughly enjoyed all the subjects and graduated with an excellent grade as listed on my resume. My enthusiasm and academic performance is also supported with the work experience I have completed at my time with Artisan where I worked as a trainee designer for over 12 months. On my resume I have also provided a link to my online portfolio.

I hope my work is of an appropriate standard for your interview requirements.

If you require any further information, please contact me, either by return mail, or on the telephone number above.

Yours Sincerely,

Samuel Nash

Example 1 Resume: Insurance Manager

William Smith
1566 Circle Street
Los Angeles, Ca
(719) 555-5632

SKILLS SUMMARY Almost 20 years' management experience in the insurance industry. With background in auditing, product management and computer system management. Skilled in developing and implementing training programs.

EMPLOYMENT HISTORY

January 2007-present

National Insurance Company
Mobile, AL
Premium Audit Manager (August 2004-present)

- Audit commercial book of business, including adjusting classifications and exposure.
- Communicate directly with independent agents to resolve audit disputes, which have enhanced working relationships between corporate office and field staff.
- Hire and train new staff on auditing guidelines and procedures.
- Supervise staff of five auditors and four support personnel.

Senior Staff Specialist, Product Management (March 2003-August 2004)

- Integrated Underwriting System into Product Management Department, which involved evaluating and placing personnel in appropriate positions.
- Maintained "common" screens for Commercial Automated System.

Systems Manager (January 1997-November 2000)

- Developed first commercial online policy issuing system for corporation
- Implemented commercial online policy system in 15 divisions and three service centres.
- Developed training program and trained support personnel to maintain and enhance system

YX Insurance Company
Mobile, AL
Casualty Staff Specialist (April 1994-January 1997)

- Handled general liability, worker's compensation and crime rates, rules and forms for all operating states
- Developed manuals to support rates, rules, forms and underwriting systems.
- Supervised staff of six

Commercial Policy Service Manager, East Divisions (May 1991-April 1994)

- Managed all commercial rating, statistical coding and policy typing, representing more than $85 million premium dollars.
- Developed and implemented training program for commercial underwriting division.
- Supervised staff of 90.

EDUCATION - University of Alabama

ACTIVITIES – Organizer of Sports Events

Example 2 Curriculum Vitae: Marketing Manager

Stephen Alexander
321 Berenedo Avenue Sacramento, CA 90089
(209) 123-4567

SKILLS SUMMARY

More than 15 years marketing experience with insurance and benefits. Experienced in developing products and programs across corporate lines. With background in developing products for benefits program.

CAREER HISTORY

Vice President-Marketing, XYZ, Inc., Princeton, NJ (May 2003-current) Senior marketing officer for general insurance underwriter. Handle marketing and sales of all product lines. Manage all personnel and functions for all five branches.

- Established new distributed system to increase flexible benefits software and administration sales, while realizing revenue from related individual product sales.

Manager-Corporate Sales, ABC Insurance Company, New York, NY (February 1999-May 2003)

Managed sales in large corporation market, primarily through brokerage sources, by taking advantage of emerging market opportunities.

- Created innovative programs for corporate markets, such as integrating group and individual products, which helped expand client base.
- Expanded number of brokerage outlets and increasing production from current brokers through relationship marketing, seminars and advertising.

Manager-Marketing, XXX Insurance Company, New York, NY (June 1997-February 1999)

Managed all marketing functions for 20 agencies and 500 agents, including advanced sales, training, payroll deduction plans, product promotion and incentives. Managed a staff of 25 and a $6 million budget.

- Introduced and edited agency newsletter, which provided sales/ marketing information, helped close communication gap between home and field offices and provided consistency in information.

Manager-Marketing Operations, PV Insurance, Philadelphia, PA (May 1993-June 1997)

Managed all sales support areas, including advanced sales, management recruiting, training and conventions, for independent brokerage. Supervised staff of 15 and $1.5 million budget.

- Designed and launched six major new products in three years, generating 1986 premium revenue of more than $50 million.

Supervisor-Product Sales, Pennsylvania Life, Philadelphia, PA (June 1982May 1983) Supervised advanced sales, product promotion and incentive program. Worked with 800 field agents. Handled all communication with field staff. Supervised office staff of three.

- Established incentive program for two new products, which generated premium revenue of more than $5 million.
- Initiated new marketing team, which designed short-and ling-term goals for all life products.

EDUCATION

B.S., Business Administration, University of Kentucky, Louisville, with honors (1982)

MEMBERSHIP

Association for advanced Life Underwriting (AALU)

National Association of Life Underwriters (NALU)

Example 3 Curriculum Vitae: Executive Administrator

Alex Mayers * 123 West Circle Drive * New York, NY 13754 * (819) 123-4567

Summary of Qualifications

More than 10 years' experience in executive administration, marketing and sales management. With background in office computer operations, office administration and training.

Professional Experience

XYX Commercial Air Filters, Oklahoma City, OK Executive Administrator, North American Products Group (August 2004-current)

Provide administrative and advisory support for corporate president and all international/regional vice presidents

- Coordinate and implement international corporate projects, policies and procedures.
- Implemented standardized office computer operations and software for domestic operations.

Executive Assistant, ABC & Consumer Group (February 2002-August 2004)

Handled administrative and advisory support for corporate president. Coordinated progress reporting and assignments of vice presidents. Planned and coordinated arrangements for all corporate meetings.

- Developed orientation and training program for administrative secretaries, which increased efficiently and productivity and reduced overlapping duties.
- Managed marketing and promotion of automotive racing program, which produced high name recognition for corporation domestically and abroad.

Marketing Assistant, ABC & Consumer Group (November 1999-April 2002)

Served as corporate assistant to consumer and automotive marketing vice presidents, national sales managers and senior product managers. Provided marketing support to 200-member sales force. Assisted in promoting automotive racing program.

- Compiled and analyzed sales/marketing reports. Oversaw new product implementation and supervised customer inquiries.
- Implemented new competitive analysis procedure, which helped establish short and long-term corporate marketing goals.

Marketing Professionals International, Tulsa, OK Program Administrator-Affiliate Services

(July 1986-November 1989)

Provided administrative support management for 15,000-member trade organization. Supervised all programs undertaken by 100 affiliated organizations. Handled public speaking membership development, convention and program planning, trade show coordination, and printing and advertising for all marketing promotions.

- Increased membership 25% in two years.

Education

Bachelor of Science in Business Administration, Tulsa State College, Tulsa, OK (1986)

- Concentration in Administrative Management

Words of Wisdom:

"We are the change we have been waiting for"

Barack Obama (44th President of United States America)

CHAPTER 13

Understanding the Interviewer

Welcome to Chapter 13 and let me commend you on your persistence and dedication.

Psychology and personality types form some very important parts of any interview. We must be aware that our interviewer is only human and therefore not completely objective in his or her thinking. They are influenced by their psychology or their perception, which is how they see the world. Their psychology is in turn affected by their personality. We must as masters at interviews be able to identify which type of personality a person has and then adjust our behavior to gain the best possible outcome for ourselves. We must understand that 'people buy from people', that is to say that likeability forms a large part of how successful we will be during the interview. Likeability is often based upon how well we get along with an individual or more specifically how well we match their personality. If we are able to get this correct we have a much higher chance of success within the interview. So what we must do is to identify early on the personality type of the interviewer and then act appropriately. I have identified for you the predominant personality types which you are most likely to encounter within an interview and also how you must approach them. Study each one and memorize them, practice each personality as a character within your role-plays before the interview so that you are ready. Be aware that these are only guides and you may sometimes encounter interviewers with a combination of personality types in which case you may have to adapt your behavior as appropriate.

Type 1: The Young Interviewer:

Typically, this interviewer is young, energetic; he or she will have a high energy cheerful and positive demeanor. You should approach the young achiever with a 'down to earth' demeanor. You should approach them with conversation which may relate to activities focused outside of work to get them onside, examples will include sports, music and social events. Your aim with this interviewer is to get them onside by establishing common interests to show them how similar you are. Remember that our Type 1 interviewer is likely to be inexperienced so ask lots of questions and guide them slightly. Being young they will likely be very enthusiastic and therefore you should also replicate their enthusiasm. High energy will be important and also positive enthusiasm regarding the company and show a drive and optimism about your future career. Remember we must relate to them in a way that mirrors their level of enthusiasm so be as keen as they are but not too much so that they view you as competition. Establish quickly that although you are similar you view them with respect. If you are older than the interviewer does not mention this or make it an issue but instead show that you are fun as well as serious and are able to seek their level.

Type 2: The Focused Businessman:

This interviewer is extremely serious and to the point, small talk will be minimal. You will need to approach this type of personality with a confidence that shows you are comfortable being business-like. You must resist the urge to lighten up the conversation by making jokes and talking about extracurricular activities unrelated to work. Instead you must discuss your academic achievements, this shows your dedication and self-discipline, these are the attributes that a Type 2 can relate to.

Emphasize your attitude to hard work, staying late and coming in early, focus also on your desire to complete your work to a high standard. Emphasize quality and precision, associate yourself with these qualities and the Type 2 will begin to loosen up slightly as he/she realizes how well you will fit into his/her organization. It will do you good to also focus on the industry as a whole and how the company relates to it, showing the breadth of your knowledge and maturity.

Type 3: The Boring Stiff

This interviewer is usually identified easily by his clothing which will be bland and simplistic. He or she is methodical, work orientated and a slight recluse. Remember that the Type 3 is not a fan of extravagant behavior or exhibitionism. They will detest over enthusiasm and too much energy. When encountering a Type 3 you should be very precise and clear. Slow down your speech slightly. The Type 3 personality is very analytical and a thinker, therefore be very focused in your responses and do not stray from the questions. They love details and therefore you need to give them plenty of information. Focus on your achievements and mention academia, they will respond positively to detail and complexity.

Type 4: The Intimidator

This interviewer is extremely serious, very conservative and organized. They are professional and take their profession as seriously as they take themselves. They will without a doubt expect the same from you. Notice the lack of initial "chit chat" and how quickly they get down to business. Watch as they ask you question after question in quick succession and dig deep into your answers, continually probing. You need to approach the Type 4 with a quiet but focused attitude, listen carefully to his/her question and respond as accurately as possible. Your physiology should mirror that of a focused professional, straight back, clear speech and full eye contact. We are not aiming to get into an intimidation match here, however ensure that the Type 4 is able to perceive your poise. Be succinct and to the point. Avoid false friendliness and being over talkative. Remember that the Type 4 doesn't want to be your friend, they want to get down to business.

Type 5: The Verbal Diarrhea

The Type 5 is the interviewer that simply cannot stop talking. He or she will likely be full of energy and very upbeat. A Type 5 will be enjoying your company as they love to communicate and they enjoy the company of people. You should establish a personal connection with them based on some similar view, work ethic, interest or enthusiasm for the chosen field. Smile and laugh and makes a joke or two if you can. Incidentally, it is always a good idea to have at least one comical story or joke in the back of your mind. Keep them talking by asking questions. They really want to talk about themselves and their work. Try to seem very interested in what they say and encourage them to talk more. Remember to keep them interested in the interview as they are usually the types who bore easily.

Words of Wisdom:

"You must have a vision and not just a vision but you must have a plan that would make you fulfil that vision."

Aliko Dangote

CHAPTER 14

Negotiating Your Pay

There is an old saying "you get what you ask for". I don't mean to be cynical, but the truth of the matter is that an employer will attempt to pay you as little as possible in exchange for as much work as possible. This is the simple truth of maximizing profits which at the end of the day is the primary motivation of a business. This is also the key strategy in gaining the maximum productivity out of your employees, by creating a financial hunger within them and therefore a willingness to work hard. In reality one of the main reasons for us seeking new employment is to generate a good income. With this in mind it would be prudent for us to make a study of how we can gain the best pay for our time and hard work. You can maximize your pay by slick negotiation and strategy. Mark well these strategies my friends because they will save you time and minimize stress.

There are two key principles to bear in mind to negotiate our pay:

1) Always negotiate from a position of power. To elaborate, simply asking for more money rarely works, all negotiation must be based on the fundamental law of exchange, which is to say simply "if you promise me increased pay then I can promise you.... (fill in the blank) .... in return.
2) Only negotiate with the power structure that controls the purse string or finances of the business/company.

When obtaining employment, it is always a good idea to leave the subject of money or pay to the last possible stage, ideally just before you have been offered the job or when you have obtained the employment, but before your pay grade has been formally agreed in the form of a contract. Remember that once you have appropriated the position of being the last and final candidate it would at this stage be extremely expensive for the company to begin the whole selection process over again for the sake of a few thousand dollars. At this late stage it would be better and more cost effective for the company to submit to your demands, so here you now have the power and leverage on your side. This is the time to demand very persuasively what you want. Just be clear to remind them of the benefits you will bring to the organization as a result.

Words of Wisdom:

"the best move you can make in negotiation is to think of an incentive the other person hasn't even thought of—and then meet it".

Eli Broad

CHAPTER 15

70 Questions the Interviewer May Ask You

Welcome to chapter 15 and again I commend you on your motivation and persistence. The more information we are able to absorb and then put into practice the more our chances of success increase. We have looked at the interview stages in some of the other chapters but our focus here is to prepare ourselves for absolutely any line of questioning that the interviewer or employer can approach us with. However, remember that at this stage time is on our side and we know that the prospective employer will simply not have enough to time continue with an extensive line of questioning around ourselves, our work experience and qualifications. They have a limit and will need to conclude the interview at some point.

Through research it has been discovered that there are only about 70 questions that it is possible to be asked and that any question asked will be a variant of these basic 70. It may sound like a lot of questions but please bear in mind that once we have the answers ready, we are in control. Therefore, I present to you now the 70 most frequently asked questions in the interview process, our objective is to prepare an answer for each and practice responding. Typically, these questions will consist of enquires that relate to you background, experience and personal qualities. Below is a list of likely questions that you will need have the answers to before, during and after your interview.

1. Why do you want this job?
2. Tell me about yourself?
3. Why should we hire you, list your qualifications and experience?

4. What do you regard as you most major achievement?
5. What do you consider yourself very good at doing?
6. What are your strengths?
7. What are your weaknesses?
8. What do you know about our organization?
9. What skills do you appreciate in a manager?
10. What do you look for in a subordinate or colleague?
11. How do you manage your day?
12. What interests you most in your work?
13. What have you read recently that has taken your interest?
14. What do you do in your spare time?
15. In what environment do you work best?
16. What motivates you?
17. If you could change your current job in anyway how would you change it?
18. How have you changed over the last five years?
19. Where do you see yourself in five years?
20. Describe a time when you felt that you were doing well.
21. Describe a time when you thought that you were not doing well.
22. What contributions do you make to a team?
23. What would your colleagues say about you? 2
4. How would your boss describe your work?
25. Tell me a time when you successfully managed a difficult situation at work.
26. When were you most happy at work?
27. Describe how you typically approach a project.
28. On holiday what do you miss most about your work?
29. What do you think you can bring to this role/job?
30. What do you think you can bring to this company?
31. Why did you leave or want to leave your current position?
32. If we asked for a reference what would it say about you?
33. What sort of salary are you expecting?
34. What do you believe is your market value and why?
35. Do you like working in a team or on your own?
36. What have you learnt in your present position? 3

7. What did you learn from your current company?
38. If you did not have to work what would you do and why?
39. Given the achievements within your resume/C.V. why was your pay so high/low?
40. What will you do if you don't get this job?
41. What other jobs have you applied for recently?
42. What decisions do you find easy to make?
43. Which decisions do you find it difficult to make?
44. How does this job fit into your career plan?
45. How long do you plan to stay with this company?
46. From your Resume / C.V. it would seem that you move every few years, why is this?
47. When do you plan to retire?
48. What training courses have you been on?
49. What training have you had for this job?
50. Which of your jobs has given you the greatest satisfaction?
51. How do you respond under pressure?
Can you give me a recent example?
52. What support or training will you need to do this job?
53. What will you look forward to in this job?
54. What sort of bonus or commission are you expecting?
55. Why were you made redundant /let go/fired?
56. Do you have children or family commitments; how will this affect your work?
57. What sort of salary are you expecting?
58. What do you think is your market value and why?
59. On a scale of 1 to 10, with 10 being the highest, how important is your job to you?
60. How did you get your last job? How did you find out about it?
61. Why were you transferred/promoted?
62. Why do you think you will do well here?
63. What questions have you for us?
64. How did you get into this line of work?
65. What is your ultimate ambition?
66. Are you prepared to work unpaid overtime and work late?

67. What do you believe sets you aside from the competition?
68. How long do you envisage staying within this position?
69. What challenges do you see ahead of you within this position?
70. Have you worked in another country or culture before?

Remember that it is not enough to simply know the answers to the questions above, we will need to practice our answers beforehand. Even if you come across a question that is not listed above it is likely to be a variation of the above so practicing speaking the answer will enable you to be more comfortable in a real life situation and adapt the answers as necessary. I hope this chapter has helped you and as always, Good Luck! You can do it!

Words of Wisdom:

"It's hard to beat a person who never gives up."

Babe Ruth

CHAPTER 16

Gaining References

Welcome my friends to Chapter 16 and I commend you on your progress so far. We will now look at the important issue of references. A reference is statement usually from a previous employer or an individual who knows you well. The idea behind a reference is that some other individual can give a recommendation that you are of good character, experience, qualification and are therefore employable. In the later stages of the employment process if we are successful we may be provided with a conditional offer. A conditional offer is a statement which basically communicates that the employer will provide you with an employment role but on the condition that the references received are adequate or positive. In a recent survey in the UK it was found that 27% of employers withdrew their job offers after receiving unsatisfactory references. Therefore, it is imperative that we also complete this part of the process to a high standard and ensure that we obtain good references.

Types of References:

Typically, there are 3 main types of reference although a prospective employer has the right to request any reference which is relevant to the role being applied for. The three types of reference are:

- Employment Reference
- Academic Reference
- Character Reference

The employment reference is typically provided by a previous employer, this will most likely have been your director, line manager or some other individual in the company that you may have reported to. The reference will likely outline the duties that you carried out, your attitude and quality of your work. The academic reference is usually provided by a previous or current educational institution that you have attended. This may be a university or an evening course or professional qualification. It is likely that your lecturer or teacher will need to produce this. The focus of this type of reference will be the qualifications that you have earned, your work ethic and conduct.

The character reference is typically provided by an individual that you know whom is considered to be trustworthy and of integrity. This could be a priest at your church, a head teacher at a local school or a magistrate. The character reference is slightly different from the previous two in that the focus is not on achievements or qualifications but on your personality traits and qualities such as honesty, thoughtfulness and wisdom. Your prospective employers may also seek information on matters including length of employment, job title, and brief details of responsibilities, abilities, and overall performance, time-keeping and about any reasons for leaving.

Applying for a reference

You will need to inform the person or the institution whom you may require a reference from in advance, be it an academic, work or character reference. You may approach them by telephone or by email or letter. It will be important to inform them of the type of position that you are applying for and in this way the referee will be able to answer some of the questions that the prospective employer may have. Do not use someone for a reference unless you have their permission. You need to be sure that you are asking the appropriate people to write a letter of reference or to provide you with a verbal reference. You also need to know what the referee is going to say about you. The best way to approach this is to ask the reference writer if they would mind if you used them as a reference. Remember to review the type of positions you are applying for with the reference giver, so they can tailor their reference to fit your circumstances.

References and the Law

In most western countries (although specific laws differ) the prospective employer also has a legal duty to ensure that the information you provide within your reference is accurate and not misleading. This means that if you have been well-discipline during your term of employment and fulfilled the expectations of someone in your role, this should appear on your reference. It also means that you can take legal action against your former employer if they deliberately or maliciously provide an accurate, negligent or misleading job reference. Whichever type of reference you receive, once you've got the job you can ask your former employer to send you a copy which is your legal right under the Data Protection Act in most western countries.

A Basic Factual Reference

Sometimes your previous employer may provide what is usually called a basic factual reference. It is quite legitimate for an employer to only provide a reference that confirms your dates of employment. This is increasingly becoming common practice and prospective employers will understand that a brief, factual reference should not be interpreted as negative. Thankfully these references are still useful in that they will still enable you to prove your past work history.

Company Reference Policy

Be aware that some past employers will not provide references, instead they will only provide job title, dates of employment, and salary history. If that's the case, be creative and try to find alternative reference writers who are willing to speak to your qualifications.

Your prospective employer should ask your permission before contacting your references. This is especially important if you are still employed at your current position as this may put you in a difficult position. It is therefore always a good idea to have three or four references available.

Preparation 1: Create a Reference List

Before you embark on making applications for your prospective job roles you should have prepared in advance a listing of the likely references. Some people like to list these on their resume / c.v. but this is not a necessary requirement, instead a simple sentence mentioning that references are available on request is sufficient.

It is advisable to create a document listing your references. You can then have this ready to provide any prospective employer who may ask either during or after the interview process. Include three or four references, along with their job title, employer, and contact information. If the employer asks you to email your references, paste the list into the body of any email you send.

Preparation 2: Maintaining your Reference Network

It is a very good idea to keep you reference providers in touch with periodic phone calls, emails or letters. The website LinkedIn (www.linkedin.com) is an ideal way to keep your reference network up-to-do date. You never know when you might need to call upon someone.

Preparation 3: Request a Reference Letter

Every time you change employment, you should make a point of ask for a written reference from your line manager or director. This way you have prepared them for the situation in which they may be called upon to provide a reference in the future.

Example Reference:

Date: To Whom It May Concern: (or name of contact requesting reference)

John Cable worked for me as a Software Engineer from September 1, 2008 until March 23, 2013. His responsibilities included requirements gathering, analysis and design of complex web applications using a variety of technologies. During the course of his employment, John proved himself to be a dependable employee, and a hard worker, with solid problem solving and technical skills. I was always impressed by John's ability to complete the work assigned to him on time. Overall, John is a talented, hard-working employee, and I am sad to see him leave. I strongly recommend John for any mid-level development position.

Yours Sincerely,
Name
Title
Contact Number

I hope you have found this chapter useful, remember to always be prepared to provide the references upon request as this demonstrates organization and credibility and as always, good luck.

Words of Wisdom

"The quality of your life is the quality of your relationships."

Anthony Robbins

CHAPTER 17

The Pre-Interview Checklist

Welcome friends and congratulations on your continued progress and dedication.

We can all become disorganized and forgetful when the pressure is on. You may find one of these times to be just before you are about to embark on the interview itself. It would be a shame to damage your hard work and preparation by forgetting a key area. So just before we go off to interview, pass with flying colors on every question and generally impress the hell out of the interviewer we must make sure that we have not forgotten anything. Therefore, a checklist is necessary to ensure we are completely prepared every time we go into battle.

The days and hours before the interview will be the time when you may feel slightly excited or even stressed and it is at these times that it is imperative we keep a cool head and continue to be methodical and disciplined. In order to ensure that we have prepared completely, it is worth going through a short checklist either in the days prior to the interview or the hour's prior, both are usually advisable. The checklist focuses of the main areas that applicants typically forget due to increased anxiety. Some of these will seem obvious and basic, however, amazing as it may seem many applicants typically overlook more than one of them.

Look through the following checks and ensure you can answer each one.

The Checklist:

General Company Knowledge

- Do I have a good knowledge of the organizations products and or services?
- Do I know the organizations directors?
- Have I looked at the website within the last 24 hours and refreshed my memory?
- Have I chosen three facts about the company to mention within the interview?
- Am I clear on what has attracted me to the organization?

General Application Knowledge

- • Do I know which role I am applying for?
- Do I know the salary?
- Do I know the salary and benefits that I am aiming for?
- Am I clear on my career goals and aspirations?
- Have I checked on the interview invite for specific requests and prepared for them?

Dress Code:

- Have I prepared a smart suit or appropriate clothing for the interview?
- Have I polished by shoes?
- Am I wearing a watch to show I am time conscious?
- Is my clothing immaculate?

Necessary Paperwork:

As interview masters, we must always be prepared and that includes having the appropriate documentation for the interview. Below are the documents you should make sure you have at the ready should you require them.

1) Curriculum Vitae/ Resume
2) Covering Letter (the copy you sent to this particular employer).
3) Letter of Invitation to the interview
4) Company Literature
5) Examples of previous work
6) Reference contacts
7) Identification

Time and Travel:

- Do I know the location of the interview?
- Have I mapped out my route to get to the interview?
- Have I calculated the time to reach the interview and added on 20mintues for unforeseen circumstances?
- Have I printed off a map?
- Have I checked the time that the interview will commence?

State of Mind and Body:

- Have I eaten recently?
- Have I hydrated my body with adequate fluids?
- Have I abstained from alcohol for the last 24 hours to ensure clarity of thinking?
- Am I in a confident and positive state?
- Have I visualized my successful outcome?

The pre-interview checklist is not meant to be overly detailed but instead a short summary of the main key points that need to ensure you have covered. This listing is to be used one or two days before the interview or even a few hours before.

Ensure that you tick off each of the points listed before you attend the interview, to miss any would be an open invitation to failure. If you do cover off all of the points then your chances of success increase greatly, remember that most of your competition will not be using such a list so you have the advantage. Good Luck!

Words of Wisdom

> *"Nothing can stop the man with the right mental attitude from achieving his goal; nothing on earth can help the man with the wrong mental attitude."*

Thomas Jefferson

CHAPTER 18

The Interview

All of our efforts in acquiring the job role of our choice will eventually come down to a key stage, the interview. If we can execute the interview stage well, we will have an excellent chance of obtaining the employment role of our choice. Throughout this book we have looked at skills, actions and techniques before and after the interview that will enhance our abilities. The successful completion of the interview is imperative. I want you to be completely prepared for this stage so now we will walk through each stage of the interview and provide you with the relevant guidance.

Preparing for the Interview:

Although we have covered this in a separate chapter in more detail it is worth mentioning some very basic preparations. Before you attend the interview you will need to ensure that you have covered the following areas:

- You are physically prepared, i.e. A good night's sleep, a shower and some food and water consumed.
- You have dressed in the appropriate business attire.
- You have with you your CV, covering letter and any presentation materials required.
- You have references with you.
- You have the location map and know how long it takes to get there.
- You know the names of the interviewers you are meeting with.

It is also imperative that you have prepared for the questions and your answers and examples that will form the majority of the interview. You should have read through the relevant chapters of this book to ensure you are 100% ready before you attend any interview.

Travelling to the interview:

When travelling to the interview there are a few important points. Firstly, ensure you are aware of the time of the interview and how long it will take to get there. It is best to choose the fastest mode of transport and the one least likely to have incidents of delay. Also ensure that you have checked the traffic report at least 90 minutes before you are due to leave. Always have your journey planned out in advance and the map of the location printed out to refer to. This will enable you to be punctual, which we must be as the first impressions count.

Arriving at the location:

Once you have arrived at the location of your interview it is imperative that you are polite and courteous to absolutely everyone that you meet. So ensure that you are of good cheer, that is to say your demeanor is pleasant and friendly. Remember that your goal is to make this location your place of employment. Therefore, everyone you meet will be associating with you on a regular basis at some point in the near future.

You must make everyone like you. This will require some acting if you are not a naturally warm and sociable person. From the cleaners to the receptionist to the interviewees themselves. It may be that later, once you have left the interview the prospective employers will ask the receptionist what they thought of you, in fact it is very likely. It may also be the case that the receptionist may make a comment to the prospective employers such as "he/she seems nice" or "he/she is rather grumpy", so we need to bear this in mind constantly. The best way to ensure you are received well is to treat everyone as if they were a member of your family or an old friend whom you like. Before you reach the interview location you may want to splash on a little perfume or aftershave. You may want to also have a mint to freshen your breath. Also remember to smile. Remember you need to walk confidently and also speak with confidence, but not arrogance. All of these visual and behavioral attributes will register subconsciously of in the minds of the people you meet. We must control what is in the minds of the people we meet by feeding them the impression of ourselves we want them to have and not the other way around.

Meeting the interviewers:

Remember that first impressions count. Behavioral psychologists estimate that humans form an opinion of someone within the first 7 seconds of meeting them. Therefore, we control how we walk, talk, the expression on our faces, the tone of our voice, our breathing patterns and our vocabulary all to our advantage. We have covered these areas in other chapters but as a short reminder it is best to do the following.

Ensure you posture is upright and that you are not slouching.

- Walk with confidence.
- Speak loudly and clearly.
- Smile often.
- Be polite.
- Initiate a handshake and ensure your handshake is firm. *
- Make sure you greet first and say that you appreciate the time they are taking to meet with you.
- Be professional in your conduct and slightly formal.

- Make some small-talk to break the ice about your journey in or the weather, but never complain.

Note: *In Islamic countries a man shaking the hand of a woman that he is not related to or married to is not permitted and vice versa.*

A likely scenario is that you will be met at the office or location of employment by a receptionist of some description. You may be asked to wait while the interviewer's come to meet with you. Make sure you a pleasant to whomever you meet. Make sure you use the bathroom if you need to. You will be met by the interviewer or you will be taken to the location in which the interview will take place and be met by the actual interviewers. This will be between one and five people. It is unusual to be interviewed by more than five people at one time. Bear in mind also that you may be interviewed more than once in the same session by different people. You will need to keep your energy levels high in this case. Treat each interview like it is the first with the same levels of enthusiasm, because for the interviewer it will be the first time.

Introducing Yourself:

It is likely that you will be seated opposite your interviewer(s) and you will need to introduce yourself and commence the interview. An agenda which outlines what will be covered in the interview may be presented to you and if so it is important that you stick to the structure. Thank them for taking the time to see you, introduce yourself and explain why you have applied for the position. Make sure that you smile (not grin) but also keep yourself business like. You may have some paperwork such as CV/ resume, presentation, information on the company and covering letter which you should have in front of you. Make sure you have a pen and note pad with you as well so that you are able to take notes. The interviewer should see that you are taking notes the entire time.

Body Language:

It is important that your body language is correct. It is important that you keep you posture upright. Use your hands to express yourself. Lean slightly forward when the interviewer is talking. Keep eye contact but do not stare, try to break your gaze occasionally. Nod your head when the interviewer is talking and also agree with the interviewer when he/she is talking. Use phrases such as "I see" and "I undertsand ", this is called active listening. Use your facial expressions to communicate, this will make you seem more friendly. Never slouch or lean back in your chair. Remember to build rapport, you should try to copy the body language of the interviewer.

Vocal Tone and Speech:

You should ensure that your speech tone is loud enough to be understood. However you should not be shouting. There will need to be a confidence in your voice, enunciate your words and be as articulate as possible. If you want to build the most rapport with your interviewer, then you may also need to mirror the vocal tone of the interviewer to a degree. If you allow the interviewer to talk first you will have some time to prepare a replication in your own voice. You will need to keep your speech speed relatively fast to show energy, vary your tone using both high and low tones to emphasize points. Do not talk too fast or too much and never talk over the interviewer.

Discussing Yourself and the Role:

You will need to have a clear story about yourself and your previous employment. You will have prepared this in advance and you should be forthcoming and enthusiastic with this information. The interviewer should not need to interrogate you to acquire information. You will need to talk openly and confidently. Ensure that you relate information with some structure in a logical fashion. Do not waffle, but be succinct and focused on the appropriate topics, do not deviate from the subject too much. When discussing your suitability for the role. Talk about you past experiences and explain why these will help with the current role. Ensure you always provide examples of past achievements. When discussing the role ensure you have a few questions ready. You may want to have these written down on a notepad in front of you.

Answering Questions:

During the interview the prospective employer will be likely to ask you some questions. I have provided you with 70 or so questions that you are likely to be asked by the interviewer in a separate chapter and you should study these and prepare your answers before attending the interview. In addition, the prospective employer may ask you to provide some evidence to back up any claims that you make and your opinion about a particular scenario to greater understand your personality. When answering any questions be sure to monitor the time you take to answer. Not too long and not too short. Maintain a good balance. Everyone becomes nervous but we must maintain our composure. The best way to do this is to slow down the pace when being asked a question you will not get any points for answering too quickly. First ensure that you have understood the question fully. You may want to repeat it back to the interviewer for clarification. Then take a breath and think about your answer before you speak. Try to gage what the interviewer is really trying to understand about you by asking the question, once you have understood what he/she wants to hear or understand then formulate calmly the answer in your mind and then speak. Always follow up your answer with a clarification. For example, "is that the types of answer you were looking for?" or "did I answer your question to the appropriate degree?" or "would you like me to elaborate further?". Remember that the point of answering any question is to tell yourself every question they ask you is a gift and opportunity for you to sell yourself.

Asking Questions:

During the interview there will be opportunities for you to ask questions concerning the company and the role. Again you should have prepared a number of questions in advance and they should be written down. You are interviewing them as much as they are interviewing you. You want to be sure that you are joining an organization with potential and opportunity for career progress. You may ask questions about the turnover of the company, stock options, benefits packages, working conditions, start times and targets. Be sure to keep your questions to less than seven because you do not want to seem overly aggressive. Seven questions should provide you with enough information to decide whether or not you would like to work at the organization. Keep the questions direct and be polite when asking, be conversational rather than going through a scripted question, you may want to ask questions as you speak to the interviewer as opposed to leaving them all to the end, this will make them seem more natural.

Concluding the Interview:

Upon the conclusion of the interview it is important too close. That is, you must clarify that you have provided the interviewer with everything that they require and then ask whether there is any reason they would not hire you. You are trying to gain some form of commitment at that time. Make sure that you thank them and shake their hand.

After Interview Correspondence:

Always thank the prospective employer in writing. Most people do not do this so it is a great way to stand out from the crowd. Send an email or better still type a letter and post it. Say how much you enjoyed meeting with them and how you look forward to their decision. You may also offer them the opportunity to speak to any references.

Words of Wisdom:

> *"Many of life's failures are people who did not realize how close they were to success when they gave up."*

Thomas A. Edison

CONCLUSION

Congratulations my friends! I am so pleased you have taken this step forward in creating your dream career. You now have all the tools that you need to successfully obtain the role of your choice. Read this book again and again, be confident and remember that any goal that can be conceived can be achieved.

Go for it!

Words of Wisdom

"The person who succeeds is not the one, who holds back, fearing failure, nor the one who never fails, but rather the one who moves on in spite of failure. Far better to dare mighty things, to win glorious triumphs, even though checkered by failure, than to take rank with those poor spirits who neither enjoy much nor suffer much because they live in the grey twilight that knows not victory or defeat."

Theodore Roosevelt

"He did it with all his heart, and prospered".

The Bible

"But those who believe and do right, will have a continuing reward".

The Quran

"Discipline is the bridge between goals and accomplishment"

Jim Rohn

"Self-discipline begins with the mastery of your thoughts. If you don't control what you think, you can't control what you do. Simply, self-discipline enables you to think first and act afterward."

Napoleon Hill

"When I let go of what I am, I become what I might be."

Lao-tzu

"Don't let the noise of others' opinions drown out your own inner voice."

Steve Jobs

"Confidence is a habit that can be developed by acting as if you already had the confidence you desire to have."

Brian Tracy